Challenging racism:

further education leading the way

The full report of the Commission
for Black Staff in Further Education

Contents

Acknowledgements

The Commission for Black Staff in Further Education wishes to thank the following people for their significant contributions to the report.

The editorial committee – David Gibson, Rajinder Mann, Chrissie Farley, Robin Landman, Bernie Borland, Dame Lorna Boreland-Kelly, Phil Barnett, Sam Allen, Joel Whittle. In particular Robin Landman for his contribution in guiding the work of the report.

Josephine Ocloo for her work as Project Director and lead writer; and Stella Dadzie and Pat Hood for joining the Commission's writing team.

The many other people who worked tirelessly on the report, especially Yasmin Prabhudas for her work as researcher and proofreader; Alison Evans, Michael Damiani, Martin Bulmer, and Tony Mahon for their assistance in data collection and analysis, and Rita Volante for administrative support.

We would like to thank the research team based at the Institute for Policy Studies in Education in the University of North London. Our thanks also go to the Learning and Skills Development Agency research team.

Finally, the Commission would like to thank all of those people who contributed to the Commission's witness events, the expert witnesses, and the further education college sector for making the work possible.

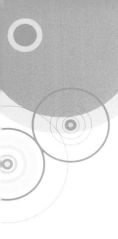

A message from the Parliamentary Under-Secretary of State for Adult Learning and Skills
Ivan Lewis MP

I am very pleased to welcome the publication of the full report from the Commission for Black Staff in Further Education and to commend it to the further education sector.

The Commission's work represents a lot of effort by a lot of people over the last couple of years and comes from the only education sector, to date, to have reviewed the working situation for its Black staff. Taking that step was not an easy one. As the report and recommendations show, you don't always get a favourable answer when you ask difficult questions.

Getting to grips with how racism impacts on the working lives of Black staff, and the organisations they work in, speaks volumes about how far the sector is willing to go to meet its challenges.

I was struck by the Commission's findings. Clearly, there's an imbalance. Yet, the findings, however commendable, represent only the first step. As lead agencies and individuals, we all have a responsibility for taking the next steps.

Put simply, we should not discriminate. We should not tolerate discrimination from others. We should not accept that our systems are fixed or cannot be improved to ensure they give everyone an equal chance.

The Commission's work and recommendations are set against a backdrop of significant change in further education. Neither the Commission nor I would wish to add any unnecessary burdens. Yet the drive for higher standards needs to tackle complacency, change attitudes, and remove the more obvious barriers to success.

Our commitment to this is no less rigorous. We will take joint responsibility with the Learning and Skills Council (LSC) to ensure the Commission's recommendations are implemented and evaluated by 2004. We will continue to champion the Commission's work. However, the government and the LSC cannot do this on their own. We need a partnership approach, building on the expertise of the Commission, and we therefore propose to convene a steering group of key stakeholders to take this work forward.

An integral part of the strategy for reforming further education must be to create a more diverse workforce, aware of its commitments to equality and opportunity and to challenging those practices that inhibit the ability of Black staff to reach the highest levels. After all, further education is in the business of creating opportunity. It offers the widest possible range of advancement to just about all comers.

These actions are only the first steps on a long journey. And that's why this report is such a landmark. At the end of the day, it isn't the Commission, the Department or the LSC that will change the situation or create opportunity. It's every person thinking, looking harder at how they do things, striving to take things further forward together. This report is a wake-up call. Once we've heard it, we can have no excuses for failing to act.

Ivan Lewis MP
Parliamentary Under-Secretary of State for Adult Learning and Skills
Department for Education and Skills

Foreword

'I have the audacity to believe that peoples everywhere can have three meals a day for their bodies, education and culture for their minds and dignity, equality and freedom for their spirits.
I believe what self centred people have torn down; other centred people can build up.'

Martin Luther King

Education should lay the foundations for a better world. The focus of this report is on the Commission's findings and recommendations for tackling institutional racism in the further education sector, thereby enabling positive role models for all sectors of our society to emerge and be sustained at all levels.

The role of education is to equip learners with the knowledge, skills and understanding to form attitudes and make choices. Anyone involved in education has a duty to help learners think critically, make informed judgements, to challenge stereotypes and to speak up for what is right. Racism is morally wrong and it needs to be addressed in all its forms. This report seeks to identify ways of tackling the under-representation of Black staff in further education, which is key to raising achievement for all learners.

In many ways, the Commission's findings are not surprising. The numbers of Black staff at different levels within the profession suggest that while progress has been made, there is still a long way to go.

The witness day accounts of individual experiences were deeply moving and often painful. Some of the deep-seated problems that Black staff face were only too evident as members of the Commission listened to people from different parts of the country. Some anonymous examples of these accounts of both poor and good practice are set out in chapter 3.

Our report and the good practice guidance that accompanies it are evidence that it is not the Commission's intention to give dedicated, hard working people in the sector yet another kick by stating what is wrong, yet offering no solutions. Quite the reverse! The Commission is encouraged by the fact that the sector is prepared to tackle this most invidious of problems and acknowledges that major progress has been made where learners are concerned. There is much good practice in the sector; colleges using this good practice must become a beacon for everyone.

The report sets out a number of issues concerning recruitment practices and race equality policies and procedures and makes recommendations that will help to take the sector forward. The landscape has changed and we needed to take account of this. The establishment of the Learning and Skills Council, the enactment of the Learning and Skills Act 2000, the Race Relations (Amendment) Act 2000, the national elections in 2001 and elections in other parts of Europe this year provide an even greater imperative to address racism. The lessons from the Stephen Lawrence inquiry have given added impetus to our work and to the legislation that followed.

The world post-11th September has become much less certain. Much thought has been given to issues of Islamaphobia and the public order disturbances in Bradford, Burnley and Oldham in the summer of 2001. What is certain is that all colleges have a role to play in ensuring that institutional racism is eliminated. The Commission has chosen to work in partnership with the sector and it is remarkable how much common agreement exists on the issues that need to be addressed. If change is to occur, the Commission must be a critical friend to the sector and participate actively in finding solutions. To this effect we have prioritised the need to address the under-representation of Black staff at senior management level. This will be advanced through a funded programme to support their professional development. Hopefully, this scheme can be expanded in the future to support the career development of Black staff at all levels.

It is clear that the issues around equalities are complex. The witness day accounts are testament to that. Multiple discrimination factors are at play. The Commission acknowledges these, gender and disability in particular. Our remit however has been about Black staff, to make an immediate impact and to contribute to the debate about getting enough Black staff in Further Education. Changes in best staffing practice to include an element on race and equalities in Investors In People will also help.

This report is dedicated to those who have helped to take forward the struggle for social justice and for the dignity of Black staff, especially those people who trusted us enough to come and give their accounts during the Commission's witness days, in the hope and expectation that their evidence would help to make a difference. We are confident that assertive action by everyone will ensure that our shared goal of eliminating discrimination and promoting race equality is achieved.

Michael Peters
Chair, Commission for Black Staff in Further Education
October 2002

Chapter 1

Setting the context

1.1   Introduction

'The Further Education sector is key to improving the United Kingdom's workforce, skills and economic competitiveness'.[1]

Chief Executive, Learning and Skills Council

Further education colleges play a critical role in advancing the learning revolution, delivering more than 40% of entrants into higher education and transforming choices both for adult learners and the 14-19 age group.[2] They also play a vital part in `supporting current efforts within higher education to widen access to students from the poorest backgrounds. In this context, the Department for Education and Skills (DfES) has emphasised consistently the sector's importance in realising the government's ambitions of increasing workforce skills, improving productivity, and reducing social exclusion by targeting vulnerable groups.[3]

The government's endorsement of the sector is warmly welcomed by all the key stakeholders. However, the Commission believes it is essential that the current funding concerns of managers and unions are addressed. The Association of Colleges (AOC) has pointed out that no other education provider has experienced the 1% year on year cuts in core funding which have taken place within the further education sector since 1993.[4] Whilst a lack of funds cannot be seen as an excuse for inaction in promoting equality, the Commission recognises that colleges must be adequately resourced if they are to achieve the government's ambitious goals and make the essential changes outlined in this report's recommendations.

To play their part in improving the national economy, colleges need a skilled and motivated workforce that is representative of the diverse, multi-racial nature of British society. However, the sector is currently experiencing a crisis in recruiting and retaining staff. In 2001, the *Times Educational Supplement* reported that colleges faced their worst ever recruitment position, with 70% experiencing problems recruiting teachers, managers and support staff at all levels. Recent research suggests that low salary levels relative to other sectors, particularly schools, are having a detrimental impact on recruitment.[5] NATFHE, the university and college lecturers' union, has described the situation as particularly acute for lecturers, who are leaving the sector in increasing numbers because of low pay and demanding workloads.[6]

This recruitment crisis takes place within the context of significant under-representation of Black staff in the sector, particularly at senior management level. Whilst colleges have achieved major successes in recruiting Black learners, they have yet to match this success in their recruitment of Black staff. The proportion of minority ethnic students in colleges in England has increased from 12% in 1997-98 to 14% in 1999-2000, but there has been no parallel increase in the numbers of Black staff.

Only 1% of further education colleges currently have a Black principal, representing four out of 412 mainstream colleges in England, including 107 sixth form colleges. This level of under-representation of Black staff is not

unique to further education. Under-representation in public service has been highlighted as a significant issue in a recent report produced by the Institute for Public Policy Research, 2002.[7] The report argues for a change in the law to allow quotas to address the low level of minority ethnic representation in elected political office. Under-representation, it argues, detracts from 'the diversity and representative nature of our democratic institutions'.

The importance of a diverse workforce was illustrated equally forcefully by the outcome of the Damilola Taylor murder inquiry. Agencies responsible for overseeing justice in the Damilola Taylor case were criticised heavily for their 'deep, systemic failure to discharge their duty with even bare adequacy'. When the Metropolitan Police Commissioner, Sir John Stevens, responded that his force found it difficult to talk to the people on the estate where Damilola was killed, *The Times* argued that 'Sir John speaks for a force still struggling to recruit officers diverse enough to reflect modern London and sufficiently attuned to all its communities to gather the evidence necessary to see justice done. For reasons of efficiency in crime-fighting, not political correctness, the Met must quickly develop a much more diverse recruiting base'.[8] This message is also true for colleges.

Under-representation is often explained by locating the problem within Black communities, or by suggesting that individuals lack key skills and experience. Yet research shows that Britain's minority ethnic communities are often better educated than White ethnic groups. Despite this, most Black workers are paid significantly less than their White colleagues, and are the first to be sacked in a recession.[9] Research also shows that graduates from Black and minority ethnic groups have significantly lower employment rates than White graduates.[10] This untapped potential needs to be fully utilised if the sector is to achieve equality and diversity in the workforce, thereby empowering all learners to participate and achieve.

The tragic deaths of Stephen Lawrence and Damilola Taylor demonstrate the urgency for all public organisations, including colleges, to accept that diversity in employment and service delivery is not optional, but a necessary part of achieving organisational goals. As well as the persuasive business case for tackling racism, there is a moral imperative for the sector to take a lead. Further education is committed to inclusiveness and prides itself on attracting a wide and varied group of individuals. Colleges play an important part in the moral and social lives of their communities. Promoting good race relations, tackling unlawful discrimination, and removing barriers for Black staff must be part and parcel of their mission.

1.2 The Commission for Black Staff in Further Education

Aims

The Commission for Black Staff in Further Education was established following recommendations from the Stephen Lawrence Inquiry Report in 1999[11] to work in partnership with the sector to:

- challenge racism

- break down barriers for Black staff

- raise the achievement level of all who work and learn in further education.

Sponsors

Key organisations in the sector recognised the pressing need to tackle institutional racism and established the Commission as an independent body. Sponsor organisations included the AOC, NATFHE, the Network for Black Managers and the Learning and Skills Council (LSC).

As work progressed, other organisations expressed a wish to contribute. They included the Sixth Form Colleges' Employers' Forum, UNISON, the public service union, the Association for College Management and the GMB, Britain's general union.

Funding

The Commission's work is funded by the DfES and the LSC up to January 2003. The Commission agreed that its work must be practical and time limited, and focused on securing workable recommendations both for the sector as a whole, and for individual stakeholder organisations.

Terms of reference

The Commission's terms of reference were to examine:

- the current employment profile of Black staff in further education

- factors that might dissuade Black people from entering careers in further education and those that encourage them to work in the sector

- institutional factors that might undermine Black staff

- institutional factors that might inhibit the progression of Black people throughout the sector

- practices in recruitment and selection.

Terminology

The Commission's use of the term 'Black' includes members of African, African Caribbean, Asian and other visible minority ethnic communities who may face racism. However, the Commission is conscious that debate about terminology continues to develop.

1.3   The Commission's approach

Methodology

The Commission approached its work by:

- gathering first-hand evidence from individuals

- commissioning the production of quantitative and qualitative data about the involvement of Black staff in the sector

- receiving evidence from national organisations, key stakeholders and expert witnesses

- holding events at which groups of Black staff were encouraged to express their views.

Witness evidence

Both qualitative and quantitative evidence informed the Commission's research and its analysis of how racism operates within the sector. The Commission took evidence from a series of ten 'witness day' events held throughout the country between 2000 and 2001 (see appendix A). Some 200 staff from all backgrounds spoke of their experiences and gave their views on what could be done to tackle under-representation, discrimination and other concerns. Many of the witnesses described how discriminatory policies, practices and attitudes in colleges impacted upon their working lives. Their examples ranged from accounts of subtle stereotyping, which trapped them in jobs with little hope of progression, to overt bullying and harassment. The events helped raise commissioners' awareness of how race equality policies and practices in the sector impact upon the professional lives and experiences of Black staff.

Commissioned research

A national survey was carried out by the University of North London between May 2001 and April 2002 to assess the employment position of Black staff. The national survey data comprised statistical evidence as well as qualitative data from interviews and focus groups in eight case study colleges. The national survey reaches important conclusions about the numbers of Black staff in further education, the positions they hold and the levels of discrimination they may face. The data contributed to the Commission's analysis of the effectiveness of equal opportunity and race equality policies within the sector.

Other sources of evidence

Data from the LSC's recently published Staff Individualised Records (SIR) for 2000-2001 and the Individualised Student Record (ISR),[12] Labour Force Survey data for 2000-2001,[13] as well as information from research into recruitment and selection practices conducted by the Learning and Skills Development Agency (LSDA) in 2002[14] contributed to the evidence base. The Commission also sought evidence from expert witnesses, national organisations and agencies.

Establishing a definitive picture of the sector

Collating the research evidence was challenging and issues arose as the Commission tried to gain a full and consistent picture. Issues about data collection and consistency have been a feature of the Commission's concerns from the outset. It was vital to have a reliable database in monitoring race equality in employment and service delivery. An earlier pilot survey carried out by the Commission identified difficulties within colleges in supplying data on ethnicity. Both the LSDA and national survey research were unable to gain full returns regarding the numbers of Black and White staff in colleges. In the national survey, 48% of colleges provided a valid response to the questions on Black and White staff numbers (compared with 25% in the LSDA research). Whilst this is a good response for a postal survey, it still raises questions about the situation in non-responding colleges. Given the difficulties in supplying precise figures, colleges were asked to give their best estimates of the numbers of Black and White staff. More issues arose when the Commission tried to establish a clear picture of staff in senior positions (see chapter 2 for further details). The LSC data provided important supplementary evidence; however valid returns for 2000-2001 were only available for 291 colleges. As a result, the LSC used SIR data from previous years for a further 117 colleges to produce a full dataset. This data is broken down into certain staffing categories, however it does not include specific and discrete information on staff in management positions. Colleges are only required to supply ethnicity data for those staff who work 25% or more of a full-time post.

The Commission was keen to use a variety of approaches to seeking evidence about the employment position of Black staff, in order to fill as many gaps as possible in the available datasets. The picture presented in this report makes an important contribution to information available already. There is a pressing need for a consistent method of data collection in colleges so that future analysis is easier and accurate.

Interim findings

The Commission presented its initial findings at a consultative conference in Birmingham in October 2001. Representatives from the further education sector, including governors, principals, managers, lecturers and support staff, among them many Black staff, heard speakers discuss how the sector could most effectively tackle institutional racism. Their message was that change was long overdue, and that the responsibility lay with all bodies – from the DfES, the LSC, the Adult Learning Inspectorate (ALI) and the Office for Standards in Education (OFSTED) to college corporations, principals, senior managers and staff.

1.4   The legal and statutory context

The current framework

The Commission makes its report within a framework of supportive national legislation. Colleges, in common with other public sector bodies, now have a duty to be proactive in their approach to race equality. The new duty complements existing legislation which makes direct and indirect discrimination on racial grounds unlawful. It also allows for positive action, in

the form of discrete and specific measures, for particular groups in order to compensate for longstanding social and economic disadvantage linked to discrimination.

The Race Relations (Amendment) Act 2000

The Race Relations (Amendment) Act 2000 came into effect on 2nd April 2001. It extends protection from unlawful racial discrimination in a number of key aspects of service delivery by the public sector and places a new enforceable duty on listed public authorities to have due regard in everything they do to the need to:

- eliminate unlawful racial discrimination
- promote equality of opportunity
- promote good relations between people of different racial groups.

The three duties are complementary and each needs to be acted on in relation to all the relevant functions of a public authority. The new law requires all public authorities listed in Schedule 1A of the Act, including further education colleges, to adopt a systematic and proactive approach to meeting these duties. The Act allows the weight given to a particular function or policy to be proportionate to its relevance to race equality.

Positive action, as defined in the Race Relations Act (1976), remains an important device, under-used by colleges, for addressing racial inequalities; and constitutes the only lawful means to tackle the under-representation of Black staff in employment, training and on governing bodies.

Specific duties

In order to help colleges meet the general duty, the Home Secretary has placed a number of specific duties on further education colleges. These are:

- to prepare a written race equality policy (by 31st May 2002)
- to assess the impact of policies on students and staff from different racial groups
- to monitor the admission and progression of students and the recruitment and career progression of staff by racial group
- to include arrangements in the written race equality policy for publishing the results of assessment and monitoring
- to take steps to publish the results of monitoring and impact assessment.

The LSC is required to publish annually an analysis by ethnicity of further education teaching staff. Colleges will have to ensure they are able to collect and report such data.

Statutory code of practice

The Commission for Racial Equality (CRE), which has powers to enforce the Act's duties, has published a statutory code of practice to guide implementation of the Act. The provisions of the code can be taken into account in legal action that may be taken against a college under the Act. Advice to colleges on complying with the Act is also available from regional CRE offices and local race equality councils. Further information is included in the *Framework for a Race Equality Policy for Further Education Colleges*[15] and can be obtained from the CRE website, *www.cre.gov.uk* (see appendix B).

Compliance

The LSC is also bound by the general duty and is subject to a set of specific duties that enable the general duty to be met. The LSC's duty with regard to further education colleges is to ensure their compliance with the duties placed on them. However, governing bodies of colleges are legally responsible for their compliance and are liable if there is a breach of the law.

The costs of discrimination

By 'race equality proofing' their functions in a systematic way, colleges will be contributing to an equalities infrastructure that makes it easier for them to comply with the broad range of anti-discrimination legislation. The Commission noted that in 2001, 3,831 people registered race bias claims at employment tribunals. This was the highest number ever recorded and represented an increase of 280% compared with five years ago.[16] The financial and human costs of tribunals remain unacceptably high. The cost of rigorously pursuing race equality standards must therefore be weighed against the cost of not doing so. It is the Commission's view that colleges cannot afford to contribute to the devastating impact of unfair discrimination and harassment upon individuals and society. Neither can they afford to ignore the significant implications for efficiency, productivity and organisational competitiveness resulting from discriminatory employment practices.

The LSC equalities remit

The LSC is responsible for funding all post-16 education and training and has an important role to play in championing and mainstreaming equality. The Council has a statutory duty to have due regard to the need to promote equality of opportunity between: people from different racial groups; men and women, and people with a disability and people without. The Act requires the LSC to report annually to the Secretary of State on:

- equality arrangements it has made during the preceding years
- the effectiveness of the arrangement
- equality and diversity plans for the following year.[17]

The Secretary of State requires that the LSC promotes equal opportunities throughout its work, both internally through its personnel policies and externally by embedding equal opportunities in all its policies, programmes and actions. The LSC's Corporate Plan 2001 and National Equality and Diversity Strategy[18] set out how the Council intends to meet the requirement.

1.4.8 Other relevant legislation

Other relevant legislation with which the LSC and further education colleges must comply includes:

- the Special Educational Needs and Disability Act (SENDA) 2001 which amends the Disability Discrimination Act (DDA) 1995

- the Sex Discrimination Act 1975

- the Human Rights Act 2000

- forthcoming European legislation outlawing discrimination in employment and training on the grounds of age, sexual orientation, religion or belief.

1.5   Mainstreaming

'Mainstreaming builds equality openly and actively into policy-making processes at all levels and at all stages. It ensures that policies, programmes and actions specifically seek to achieve equality, and do not put any group of people at a disadvantage, mainstreaming identifies where special measures are needed. The aim is to provide equal opportunities for everyone in the community.' [19]

Equal Opportunity Commission's Annual Report, 1999/2000

Mainstreaming equality

As well as the legislative framework, the Commission has taken account of new concepts and policy trends. Mainstreaming is an important concept promoted by all the lead agencies in the equalities field. It is central to the Race Relations (Amendment) Act 2000 and to guidance issued by key agencies, including the inspectorates, ALI and OFSTED. The aim is to embed the elimination of discrimination and the promotion of equality of opportunity and good relations by making these requirements central to, and an integral part of, the way public sector organisations operate. For colleges, this means that equality and diversity must be part of all their activities rather than a 'bolt-on' consideration.

Mainstreaming will help colleges recognise that tackling inequality and discrimination is central to the organisation's strategic goals. Action on equality must be embedded into the organisation's culture, operations and strategic priorities, demonstrating an active commitment to ensuring that all groups, staff as well as learners, can participate and benefit equally in an environment where discrimination is outlawed and diversity is promoted and valued.

The benefits of social inclusion

The moral and ethical basis for promoting race equality and social inclusion is well established in legislation and policy. It is recognised that the costs of racism to individuals, families and communities are unacceptably high. They include social exclusion, unemployment, poverty, inadequate housing, poor health, mental illness and low educational achievement. For Black employees, the costs are evident in high levels of frustration, wasted talent and energy, and low morale. Following the success of the CRE's Leadership Challenge initiative, which encouraged heads of leading industries to sign up as 'champions' of race equality, the economic rationale for including all groups fully within organisations is more widely understood. Most colleges are keen to play their part in developing an inclusive society. To help them, the LSC in its 2002-2003 strategic plan will be establishing equality and diversity impact measures relating to the recruitment, retention and achievement of learners by age, race, sex and disability. The Council will help colleges identify their contribution to meeting these measures.

The benefits of a diverse workforce

There is considerable evidence to show that inclusive organisations benefit from diversity by:

- enhanced competitiveness – attracting and retaining more competent employees who understand the needs of their clients and respect differences

- improved performance and outcomes – creating a working environment in which everyone is encouraged to perform to their maximum potential

- improved customer services – being able to reflect and meet the diverse needs of their clients

- increased market share – attracting a more diverse range of customers and improved global or international links

- enhanced people management practices – using monitoring, impact assessment, staff consultation and other strategies

- improved organisational ethics and values

- increased understanding of race, diversity and equal opportunities issues

- improved staff relations

- reduced risk of costly tribunals – complying with anti-discriminatory legislation.

1.6 Institutional racism

'The collective failure of an organisation to provide an appropriate and professional service to people because of their colour, culture or ethnic origin. It can be seen or detected in processes, attitudes and behaviour which amount to discrimination through unwitting prejudice, ignorance, thoughtlessness and racist stereotyping which disadvantage minority ethnic people.' [20]

Institutional racism

The Commission has adopted the definition of institutional racism provided in the Stephen Lawrence Inquiry Report. Debates about institutional racism

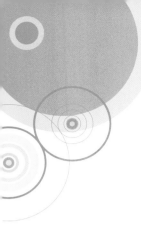

have centred mainly on whether it applies to the whole organisation or to the activities of individual 'rotten apples',[21] as suggested in the Scarman report (1981). The Lawrence inquiry helped to develop this debate by concluding that racism was institutional, structural and collective, and not simply a matter of individual prejudice, actions or behaviours. The inquiry's definition is important because it expands society's understanding of racism and rejects narrower definitions that have undermined public policy development in the past. The report singled out education as the public service best placed to make a decisive difference in the fight against institutional racism.

Findings from the Stephen Lawrence inquiry

Findings from the inquiry correspond with much of the evidence presented to the Commission and have important implications for colleges. The relevant findings concluded that:

- institutional racism could arise from overt acts of discrimination and/or hostility by individuals acting out their personal prejudices and from inflexible, 'traditional' ways of doing things, especially in tight-knit or long-standing communities

- racism was sometimes fuelled by a mistaken 'colour blind' approach where everybody is treated the same instead of recognising and responding to individual needs

- racism could be embedded in laws, customs and practices and in structures, policies and processes, resulting in allegations of institutional racism regardless of the intention of individuals

- 'unwitting' racism could arise from a lack of understanding, ignorance or mistaken beliefs; from well-intentioned but patronising words or actions; from a lack of familiarity with the behaviour or cultural traditions of people or families from Black and minority ethnic communities; and from unconscious racist stereotyping

- the culture of an organisation was an important vehicle for the transmission of negative stereotypes, views and assumptions and might pressurise individuals to conform to prevailing norms.

Investigating racism

Colleges need to investigate how institutional racism occurs if they are to tackle it successfully. Its different elements can disadvantage or exclude Black groups and individuals in a number of ways[22] for example:

- Individual/personal racism – staff or students adhering to attitudes and behaviours based on a negative pre-judgement of other racial groups.

- Cultural racism – rituals, values, beliefs and ideas that endorse notions of European, Western or White cultural superiority.

- Eurocentrism – an ethos or curriculum that stems from and is dominated by European perspectives or ideologies, making it easier to stereotype and exclude those who do not fit into the norm.

Such attitudes and beliefs may be insidious or difficult to detect. Even so, they inform the power relations that operate on an institutional level, rationalising the allocation of resources by excluding particular groups while at the same time blaming them for their underachievement.

Implications for colleges

Acknowledging and tackling institutional racism was seen to require firm leadership the Lawrence inquiry concluded. Discriminatory and socially exclusive practices continued to flourish unchecked because expectations and requirements were not made explicit, or because the issues were considered divisive or too challenging. Acknowledging and tackling institutional racism required firm leadership and 'full partnership with members of minority ethnic communities'.[23]

Principals and governors also need to be well-informed about institutional racism, and active in its elimination. They should also prioritise the need to make strategic links with representatives of minority ethnic communities.

1.7   An agenda for action

The Commission's agenda for action

By working in partnership with the sector, the Commission has developed an action agenda for change rather than simply identified problems. This report identifies priorities for action as well as the tools the sector will need to tackle them. These priorities are reflected in the recommendations set out in chapter 5.

Pilot mentoring scheme

A key priority is to tackle the under-representation of Black staff at senior management level through a funded pilot programme of support for the professional development of Black staff. The programme will provide mentoring and work placement opportunities to enable Black staff in participating colleges to gain the experience necessary for permanent senior management posts. The pilot will be delivered and evaluated by the end of March 2003. It is hoped the programme will be adopted by the new 'leadership college' once established. The Commission would also like to see the scheme expanded to support the career development of Black staff at all levels.

Agenda for action by colleges

Institutional values have a strong influence on the values of individuals and the culture of an organisation. Tackling institutional racism in the further education sector requires a regular review of college value systems. The Commission notes that some colleges have already begun this process as part of their commitment to inclusion and equality.

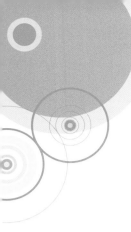
The most forward-looking, inclusive colleges are likely to be taking the following steps to promote race equality:

Leadership – the college will provide clear leadership and commitment to promote race equality. This commitment will be highly visible and feature prominently in the college prospectus, annual report (including the results of monitoring information) and other key documents.

Policy – the institution will consult widely with representatives of different ethnic groups in the college to develop a race equality policy and action plan, including discussions with trade unions.

Accountability – the college will ensure that everybody (governors, staff and students) understands their responsibility for promoting race equality.

Mainstreaming – the race equality action plan will be integrated into the college's strategic plan. Each department will have its own race equality objectives and managers at all levels will have measurable race and equality targets built into their personal appraisal plans.

Marketing – positive multi-racial/cultural images will promote the college, regardless of its ethnic composition or that of the locality.

Ethnic monitoring – the college will collect, analyse and monitor data by ethnicity annually, in a uniform way, and present this in a clear and accessible form.

Target setting – targets for race and equality will be set as part of the college's strategic plan, using key benchmarks such as the size of the local minority ethnic communities, the college's student population and the national minority ethnic population.

Positive action – positive action will provide facilities or services to meet the special needs of people from particular racial groups (for example, English language classes); job training will target particular racial groups that are under-represented in an identified area of work; and applications from racial groups under-represented in identified work areas will be encouraged.

Reviewing progress – the college will achieve steady progress by regularly reviewing and evaluating policy and progress.

Good practice guidance

A series of good practice guides has been commissioned to help the sector tackle racism. The guides cover staff recruitment, selection, retention and progression, staff development and training, and monitoring and inspection. Aimed at managers and other key staff in further education colleges, the guidance is intended both to support the Commission's findings and to promote effective practical responses to the requirements of the Race Relations (Amendment) Act 2000. The Commission regards the guidance as vital in achieving a far-reaching influence on race equality practice and positive action strategies within the sector.

Notes

1. *Times Educational Supplement* (2001) 16 November.

2. *Times Educational Supplement* (2002) 4 January.

3. HM Treasury (2002) *Developing workforce skills: piloting a new approach,* London.

4. AOC (Summer 2002) *FE Now,* The Independent.

5. ORC International (2001) *Association of Colleges and joint unions national review of staffing and pay in further education,* London.

6. NATFHE (28 May 2002) *Overworked and undervalued,* London.

7. Rushanara and O' Cinneide (2002) *Our House? Race and representation in British Politics,* London: Institute for Public Policy Research.

8. *The Times* (2002) 26 April.

9. Dickens, R, Gregg, P and Wadsworth J (2001) *The State of Working Britain,* York: York Publishing.

10. Department for Education and Employment press notice (4 April 2001).

11. Macpherson, W (1999) *The Stephen Lawrence Inquiry: Report of an Inquiry by Sir William Macpherson,* London: Stationery Office.

12. Learning and Skills Council, *Individualised Student Record 20, 2000-2001.*

13. Office for National Statistics, *Labour Force Survey 2000-2001,* London.

14. Learning and Skills Development Agency and the Commission for Black Staff in Further Education (April 2002) *Black issues in recruitment procedures and processes in the Further Education sector,* London.

15. Commission for Racial Equality (2002) *Framework for a race equality for further education colleges,* London: HMSO.

16. Labour Research Department (2002) *Labour Research,* April.

17. Learning and Skills Act 2000: 14.

18. Learning and Skills Council (2002) *National Equality and Diversity Strategy.*

19. Equal Opportunity Commission, *Equality in the 21st century, Annual Report 1999/2000.*

20. Macpherson, W, op. cit., p.28.

21. Macpherson, W, op. cit., p.22

22. Dominelli (second ed. 1998: 7) *Anti-racist social work,* London: MacMillan.

23. Macpherson, W, op. cit., p.31.

Chapter
2

Black staff in further education: the quantitative evidence

2.1   Key findings

- Black staff are under-represented in individual colleges and at local and regional levels compared with learner populations.

- Most colleges employ fewer than 5% Black staff.

- Black staff are under-represented at management and senior management level.

- Only 1% of principals are Black.

- Many college corporations have no Black governors or corporation clerks.

- Out of 134 colleges with 2178 governors, only 178 are Black.

- Black lecturing staff are over-represented in part-time, hourly paid lecturing posts.

- Proportionately fewer Black staff are on permanent contracts compared with their White colleagues.

- Black staff are disproportionately concentrated in contracted-out services.

- Black lecturers are concentrated in certain curriculum areas, particularly continuing education, which includes basic skills and English for Speakers of Other Languages and to a lesser extent in maths and science departments.

- More Black staff are educated to at least first degree level than their White counterparts.

- There are very few senior and full-time Black inspectors.

- The percentage of Black learners has increased in further education over recent years.

- Overall Black learners continue to underachieve compared with White learners.

- Most colleges have equal opportunity policies, although prior to 31st May 2002, few had developed discrete race equality policies.

- Most colleges claim to use ethnic monitoring data, but few set targets for the employment or progression of under-represented groups.

The Commission's findings are set out in full in chapter 5.

2.2   Methodology

Scope

The Commission wanted to find out how many Black staff were working in colleges, compared with the number of Black people in the overall population. It also wanted information about the levels at which Black staff work and about their qualifications. In particular, it was keen to determine the proportion of Black staff compared with the number of Black students, and whether this had any impact on the achievement of Black students.

Access to data

The evidence in this section is drawn from a range of sources and reflects the wide-ranging research carried out by the Commission. The sector does not yet have access to a uniform and reliable database on ethnicity. Considerable gaps remain in the information collected, making it impossible to establish a definitive picture of the overall staffing profile. However, by drawing on a range of data, the Commission was able to reach some conclusions about the number and position of Black staff employed in the sector. Its key findings were summarised earlier at the start of this chapter.

Staff Individualised Record

Data from the Learning and Skills Council's (LSC) *Staff Individualised Record* (SIR) for 2000-2001 and the *Individualised Student Record* (ISR) provided an invaluable source of information. Colleges are required by the LSC to provide information on staffing by completing the *Staff Individualised Record* (SIR). The information requested includes an ethnicity field. The descriptors for the ethnicity field follow those recommended by the Commission for Racial Equality, which include the categories 'other' and 'unknown'. The ethnicity field is compulsory only for staff employed on contracts representing over 25% of the full-time equivalent. For this reason, only these staff are included in the further education staff statistics that follow.

Adjustments

While the LSC receives a substantial amount of information, there are significant gaps. Data are only published on staff in three categories: teaching staff, support staff and other support staff. No discrete information is published on the ethnicity of college management, staff contracts and those in part-time positions or on staff pay. The Commission has included staff placed in the 'other' category amongst minority ethnic staff and has excluded those in the 'unknown' category from the overall totals. Data on ethnic groups are therefore presented as percentages of staff of known ethnicity. This methodology is also applied to ISR data and to Labour Force Survey data, where appropriate. LSC data published in 2002 relates to the teaching year 1st August 2000 to 31st July 2001. At the time of publication, valid SIR returns for 2000-2001 were only available for 291 colleges. Therefore to ensure a complete dataset for the sector, SIR data from previous years was used for the remaining 117 colleges. (Valid returns relate to those colleges able to supply full and correctly completed returns by the required deadline.) A number of colleges involved in the research process complained about the difficulties of providing accurate information, particularly where a large number of people were involved in compiling the data. Access to appropriate software was seen as critical. Some colleges reported that their payroll had been customised to generate the SIR report data, but that when the report was changed extensively by the Further Education Funding Council their systems were no longer compatible. This meant the report had to be compiled manually, which took a considerable amount of time. In addition, the Commission noted that although colleges undoubtedly considered this exercise important, it was not attached to funding and was therefore not audited.

National survey data

The national survey and case study research carried out by the University of North London in 2001 also provided a range of data. This study looked at further education and sixth form colleges in England and gathered data on the numbers and positions of Black and White staff as well as information about equality policies and practice within the sector. The survey was conducted between 12th June and 31st August 2001. Questionnaires were sent to 412 colleges (including 107 sixth form colleges) in England. Colleges were asked to include the numbers of all Black and White staff, both full-time and part-time, who were in post for a minimum period of four weeks during the summer term of 2001. The valid response rate of the survey was 48%. Eight colleges were also selected as case studies in order to validate the statistics and capture the day-to-day realities of staff in the sector, including the effects of racism and inequality. The data was collected through questionnaires, interviews and focus groups.

Other sources

Other sources of research that informed the Commission's findings included:

- the Learning and Skills Development Agency (LSDA) research published in April 2002 on the effect of recruitment procedures on Black staff

- evidence from key organisations including the LSC, the Further Education National Training Organisation, trade unions, the Office for Standards in Education, the Training Standards Council, the Teacher Training Agency, and government agencies such as the Home Office and the Inland Revenue

- data from the *Labour Force Survey 2000-2001*, a large scale probability sample survey of the British labour force carried out on a continuing basis and published annually – this is used by government for a variety of purposes including estimating the unemployment rate, and is one of the most satisfactory sources of information about the participation of minority ethnic groups in the UK labour market.

More details about the national survey and LSDA research can be found on the website **www.aoc.org.uk/unl.htm**

2.3   Current benchmarks: national, regional and further education staffing profiles

Baseline data

The Race Relations (Amendment) Act 2000 requires colleges and other listed public authorities to establish baseline data as part of their monitoring and target setting process. This process entails gathering external data on the workforce and service provision by racial group. An important part of this activity will be to assess service delivery and to evaluate how different groups

of learners are treated, once they are recruited. Internal benchmarks will also need to be established, to enable colleges to compare their employees by ethnicity in different departments, by salary or grades or when undergoing particular processes such as recruitment or promotion.

External benchmarks

The data in this section provides a number of useful benchmarks for establishing the general demographic picture for minority ethnic groups and their participation as employees in colleges. Data showing the numbers of learners from different ethnic groups in further education are also provided. Colleges can use these figures to assess how well their Black staff profile matches their Black learner profile.

The national profile

Minority ethnic groups[1] currently make up 7% of the total population of Great Britain (England, Wales and Scotland). The proportion of minority ethnic groups in England alone is 8%.[2]

Figure 1a shows the uneven distribution of minority ethnic groups in England in the different regions. By far the largest proportion (97%) of minority ethnic people in Britain live and work in England, with only 1% resident in Wales and 2% resident in Scotland.

Figure 1a: Regional population by ethnic group, 2000-2001

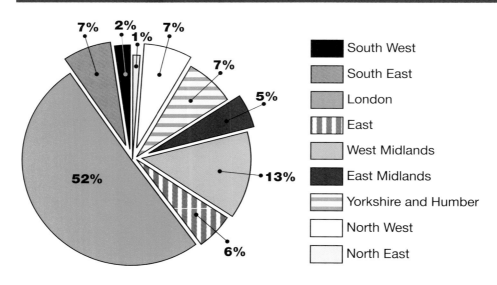

(Source: Labour Force Survey, 2000-2001)

Regional profiles

The highest proportion of people from minority ethnic groups reside and work in London and the South East, where nearly 2,000,000 people make up 28% of the population. In certain London boroughs, those from a minority ethnic background constitute a majority of the borough population. Figure 1b shows the proportion of all residents that are of minority ethnic origin in each region.

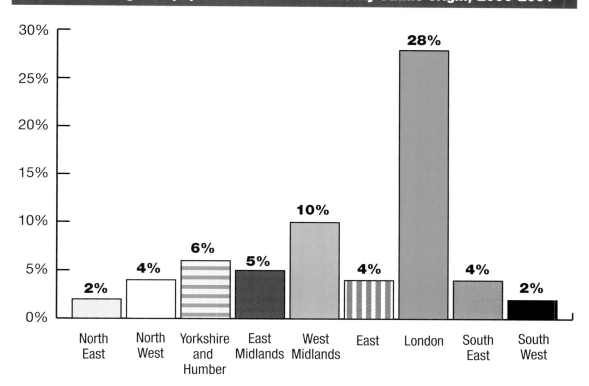

Figure 1b:
Proportion of regional population that is of minority ethnic origin, 2000-2001

(Source: Labour Force Survey, 2000-2001)

London's profile

The population composition in London varies considerably between boroughs.[3] In all but two of the London boroughs (Bexley and Havering), the minority ethnic population is higher than the 8% national average in England. In three London boroughs, the minority ethnic populations are particularly high, making up the majority of the population:

- Newham   66%
- Brent   60%
- Tower Hamlets   57%

By comparison, the smallest minority ethnic populations in London are found in:

- Bexley   5%
- Havering   6%
- Richmond   8%
- Bromley   11%
- Sutton   11%

Outside London

Outside London the minority ethnic population is unevenly distributed. At least one in five people comes from a minority ethnic group in the following areas:

Leicester	37%
Slough	32%
Birmingham	32%
Wolverhampton	26%
Manchester	21%
Bradford	21%

In other parts of the country, the minority ethnic population is significantly lower, for example:

Sandwell	18%
Kirklees	15%
Oxford	13%
Stevenage	10%
Bristol	8%
Sheffield	8%
Hull	5%
Sunderland	2%

A complete listing of minority ethnic populations in the unitary authority and local authority districts in England is provided in appendix C. These districts have been sequentially ordered according to the proportions of minority ethnic people in the population.

Black staff in further education by ethnic group

Figure 2 shows that 6.9 % of staff of known ethnicity in further education colleges in England in 2000-2001 were from minority ethnic groups.[4] Three per cent of staff in further education were African/African Caribbean, 1% were Indian, 1% were Bangladeshi/Pakistani and 2% were from other ethnic groups.

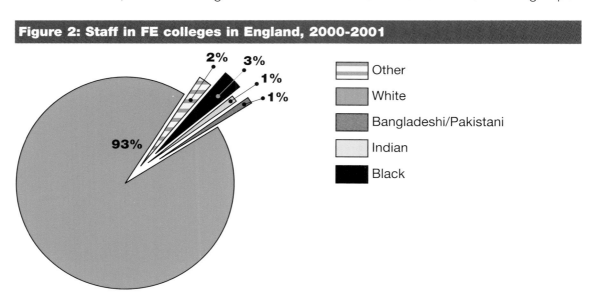

Figure 2: Staff in FE colleges in England, 2000-2001

2% 3% 1% 1% 93%

Other
White
Bangladeshi/Pakistani
Indian
Black

(Source: Staff Individualised Record, LSC, 2001)

Black staff by college function

The LSC places all staff functions, including management, into the following three categories:

- Providing teaching and promoting learning – including lecturing and preparing to teach.

- Supporting teaching and learning – for example, undertaking care assistance, providing support in a laboratory.

- Other support – for example, administration, building, maintenance and other work not related to individual students or directly to learning.

The proportion of staff from minority ethnic groups as a percentage of total numbers in each group is:

- teaching staff   7%
- support staff   6%
- other support staff   7%

These figures may give a misleading picture that all is well, but closer scrutiny suggests that this is not the case. It is important for managers and staff with responsibility for management information to appreciate the real picture revealed by the raw data.

Black principals and senior managers

There is noticeable under-representation at principal and senior manager levels with only four Black principals in mainstream further education colleges, comprising fewer than 1% of the cohort. The national survey found that Black staff constituted 4.9% of managers overall, 3.8% of heads of teaching departments and 4.6% of senior lecturers (or equivalent). White staff were more likely to be employed in managerial positions with 9% employed as managers, compared with 6.2% of Black staff. Because of the lack of a comprehensive dataset from SIR, LSDA and the national survey research, it was not possible to obtain more detailed information on Black staff in middle management and senior positions. Whilst there was clearly considerable under-representation at this level, some caution must be applied in interpreting the data set out on page 35 regarding senior postholders.

Regional variations

The regional picture, as depicted in table 3 (overleaf), shows some important variations. Black staff appear to be more evenly represented in management positions in the West Midlands (10% of Black staff compared with 9% of White staff) and also in the South East (10% of Black staff compared with 10% of White staff). However, they are under-represented in the South West (4% of Black staff compared with 7% of White staff). Of particular concern is the position of Black staff in London, who are significantly under-represented in managerial positions. Only 5% of Black staff are employed in managerial positions compared with 12% of their White colleagues.

Table 3: Percentage of Black and White staff in management positions by region

For example, 0.9% of Black staff in the North West region are senior post holders

	Nos.		Percentage of Black Staff in Further Education				Percentage of White Staff in Further Education			
	Black	White	Senior Post Holders*	Head of Teaching Dept	Head of Support Dept	Other Managers	Senior Post Holders*	Head of Teaching Dept	Head of Support Dept	Other Managers
England	**5483**	**73827**	**0.6***	**1.3**	**1.3**	**2.9**	**1.2***	**2.5**	**1.6**	**3.7**
North	49	4030	0.0*	2.0	0.0	2.0	1.6*	2.0	1.8	4.1
North West	432	14414	0.9*	1.4	2.3	2.1	1.0*	2.8	1.7	4.2
Yorkshire and the Humber	548	9863	0.5*	0.0	0.4	3.1	1.1*	1.8	1.3	3.9
West Midlands	944	10386	0.6*	3.0	1.4	5.2	1.0*	2.6	1.4	3.7
East Midlands	338	4220	2.1*	0.3	1.2	0.9	1.8*	2.2	1.5	1.6
East	534	6908	0.9*	2.2	1.1	0.7	1.3*	1.8	2.2	2.8
South West	108	6352	1.9*	0.9	0.0	0.9	1.1*	2.1	1.5	1.9
South East	513	11772	0.4*	1.6	1.6	6.6	1.1*	2.7	1.8	4.1
London	2017	5882	0.1*	0.7	1.5	2.1	1.4*	3.8	1.7	5.3

(Source: National survey, 2001)

*Senior post holders data is ambiguous as some colleges put all management staff in this category

Black staff as a percentage of the regional population

The regional picture also shows some noticeable discrepancies between the percentage of Black staff in colleges and the percentage of the Black population in different regions. Table 4 suggests there is particular under-representation of Black staff in the North West, the West Midlands and London. Surprisingly London, which has the highest percentage of Black residents, does not have a comparable percentage of Black staff.

Table 4: Percentage of Black staff compared with the population		
	% of staff who are Black	% of the population who are Black
North West	1.2	4.0
North	2.9	2.0
Yorkshire and the Humber	5.3	6.0
West Midlands	8.3	10.0
East Midlands	7.4	5.0
East	7.2	4.0
South West	1.7	2.0
South East	4.2	4.0
London	25.5	28.0
England	6.9	8.0

(Sources: National survey, 2001/Labour Force Survey, 2001)

Under-representation

The under-representation of minority ethnic groups is particularly marked when considering the proportions of Black staff in individual colleges across the regions. Figure 5 suggests that a majority of colleges employ fewer than 5% minority ethnic staff. In nearly two thirds of London colleges, the proportions of Black staff are lower than the London average minority ethnic population of 28%. Yet several London boroughs have high Black populations and 39% of learners in London are of minority ethnic origin.

Figure 5 also helps to illustrate the disparity between Black staff, Black students and local Black populations more clearly by comparing the percentage of minority ethnic people in the resident population with further education staff and the student population. It also shows the rates of Black staff in individual colleges, giving an indication of the variation that exists within each region. For example, in the East of England, 4% of the population are of minority ethnic origin: 9% of students and 7% of staff. The rates of Black staff in individual colleges range from 0% to 11%, with one college employing 23% Black staff.[5]

Figure 5: Distribution of proportions of Black staff for each college

This graph is based on the colleges that provided full staffing data in the national survey.

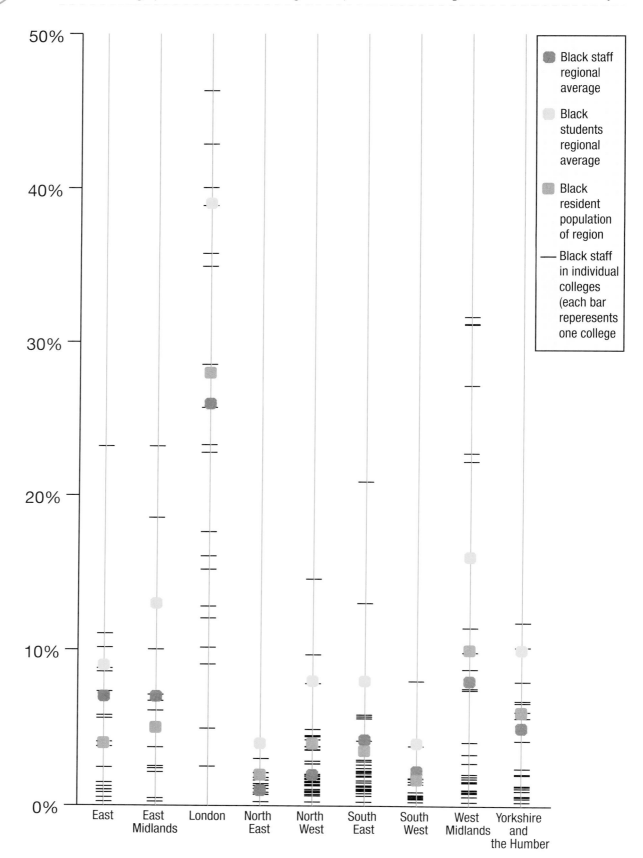

Distribution

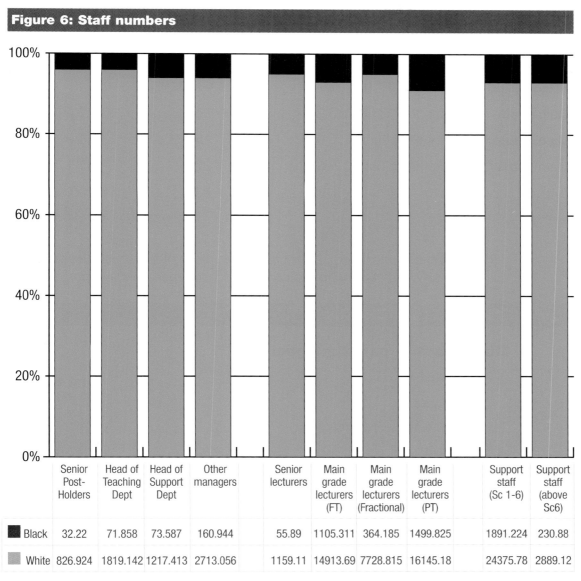

	Senior Post-Holders	Head of Teaching Dept	Head of Support Dept	Other managers		Senior lecturers	Main grade lecturers (FT)	Main grade lecturers (Fractional)	Main grade lecturers (PT)		Support staff (Sc 1-6)	Support staff (above Sc6)
■ Black	32.22	71.858	73.587	160.944		55.89	1105.311	364.185	1499.825		1891.224	230.88
White	826.924	1819.142	1217.413	2713.056		1159.11	14913.69	7728.815	16145.18		24375.78	2889.12

(Source: National survey, 2001)

Figure 6 gives an overview of the positions held by Black staff in the sector in different staffing roles and indicates that Black and White staff are unevenly distributed within further education colleges. Particular caution should be attached to the data on senior post holders. Concern over the reliability of the data arises from the way colleges defined the nature of this post in the national survey. This had the effect of over-inflating numbers of staff in this position.

Whilst Black staff are under-represented in management and senior lecturer positions, they seem to be more evenly represented in full-time teaching positions (7%) and support posts (7.2%). However, they are over-represented in part-time lecturing posts (8.5%) and under-represented in the more secure fractional posts (4.5%).

Table 7 gives a more detailed breakdown of all lecturing staff by grade and ethnicity. It illustrates percentages of Black and White lecturing staff as a proportion of the total number of lecturing staff.

Table 7: Percentage of lecturing staff who are Black and White

For example 0.1% of all lecturing staff are Black senior lecturers (2.8% of all lecturing staff are senior lecturers).

	Black (%)	White (%)	Total (%)
Senior Lecturers	0.1	2.7	2.8
Main Grade Lecturers (Full Time)	2.6	34.7	37.3
Main Grade Lecturers (Fractional)	0.8	18.0	18.8
Main Grade Lecturers (Part Time)	3.5	37.6	41.1
Total	7.0	93.0	100.0

(Source: National survey, 2001)

Table 7 complements figure 8, which illustrates these proportions in relation to all Black and all White staff in the sector, including managerial and support staff.

Figure 8: Percentage of sector staff

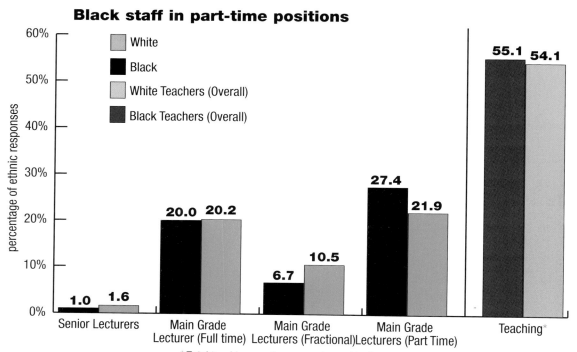

Total teaching numbers are not equal to the sum of teaching groups due to rounding

(Source: National survey, 2001)

It is evident from both datasets that compared with White teaching staff, Black staff are under-represented at all levels. Moreover, half of all Black teaching staff (3.5%) appear to be concentrated in part-time posts. This raises concerns about the ability of Black staff to secure full-time positions and the likely impact on promotional opportunities.

The concentration of Black staff in part-time positions is even greater when looking at the situation in certain regions. Table 9 depicts the ratio of Black staff in part-time positions compared with White staff, by region.

Table 9: Percentage of Black and White staff in teaching positions by region

For example, 0.2% of Black staff in the North West region are senior lecturers.

	Nos.		Percentage of Black Staff in Further Education*				Percentage of White Staff in Further Education*			
	Black	White	Senior Lecturers	Main Grade Lecturers (Full-time)	Main Grade Lecturers (Fractional)	Main Grade Lecturers (Part-time)	Senior Lecturers	Main Grade Lecturers (Full-time)	Main Grade Lecturers (Fractional)	Main Grade Lecturers (Part-time)
England	5483	73827	1.0	20.0	6.7	27.4	1.6	20.2	10.5	21.9
North	49	4030	8.2	22.4	8.2	22.4	1.1	27.4	7.6	13.7
North West	432	14414	0.2	25.2	6.0	33.3	0.9	22.8	10.6	19.5
Yorkshire and the Humber	548	9863	3.3	15.7	8.9	24.6	2.7	17.5	8.7	22.5
West Midlands	944	10386	0.2	22.8	8.6	15.8	0.7	20.4	14.1	19.9
East Midlands	338	4220	0.0	14.5	3.0	30.5	0.9	15.6	8.7	24.7
East	534	6908	1.1	16.3	5.4	48.3	2.1	22.8	7.1	18.5
South West	108	6352	2.8	13.0	0.9	50.0	2.7	19.0	7.6	29.1
South East	513	11772	0.4	16.0	5.8	27.9	1.4	18.8	14.4	20.0
London	2017	5882	1.0	22.1	6.7	25.0	2.2	17.5	9.0	33.8

(Source: National survey ,2001)

- In the East, the ratio is 48% of Black staff compared with 18% of White staff.

- In the North West, the ratio is 33% compared with 19% respectively.

- In the South West, the rato is 50% compared with 29% respectively.

This significant over-representation of Black staff in part-time teaching positions contrasts sharply with their corresponding under-representation in all other teaching grades.

Contractual arrangements

The LSC's SIR data shows that more White staff than Black staff are employed in permanent posts. Figure 10 indicates that 65% of White staff are employed on permanent contracts, compared with 60% of minority ethnic staff. It also confirms that minority ethnic staff are more likely to be employed on non-permanent contracts, with 35% of minority ethnic staff compared with 40% of White staff in non-permanent posts. (The category 'non-permanent' includes fixed-term, casual and agency teachers and teachers who are self-employed.)

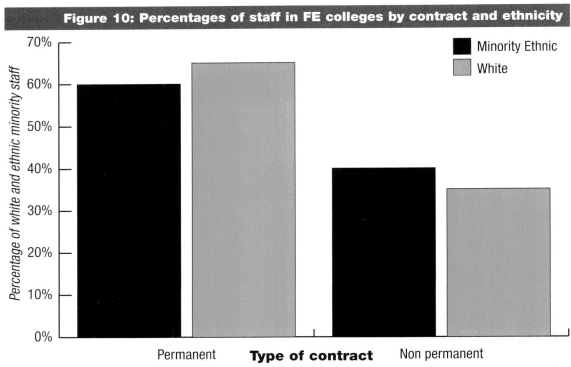

Figure 10: Percentages of staff in FE colleges by contract and ethnicity

(Source: Staff Individualised Record, LSC, 2000-2001)

The position of Black and White staff on permanent and fixed term contracts is analysed by different staff roles in the national survey research. Figure 11 illustrates that Black staff in management and teaching positions are less likely than White staff to be on permanent contracts. However, in relation to Black support staff, they are more likely to be on permanent contracts.

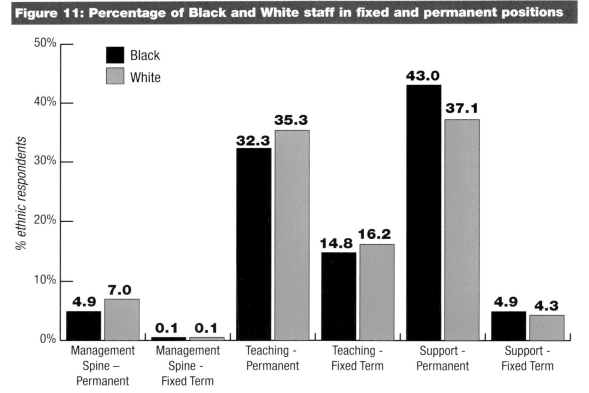

Figure 11: Percentage of Black and White staff in fixed and permanent positions

(Source: National survey, 2001)

The different approaches to data collection and the different timescales covered by the data, provide some explanation for the disparity between the national survey figures and the LSC data for the proportion of Black staff in the sector.

Qualifications

Black staff tend to be educated to a higher level than White staff overall. Figure 12 shows that 55% of minority ethnic staff in the sector are educated to at least first degree level, compared with 49% of their White colleagues.[6] In addition, 6% of minority ethnic further education staff have no formal qualifications, whereas 8% of White further education staff are similarly unqualified.

KEY: LEVEL OF QUALIFICATION

- Advanced - up to 2 A levels/OND/ONC
- Foundation - up to 4 GCSEs (D-G)
- Higher technical - up to HND/HNC
- Intermediate - up to 4 GCSEs (A-C)
- Professional - first degree, further degree and above

Figure 12: Percentage of staff in FE colleges by qualification and ethnicity

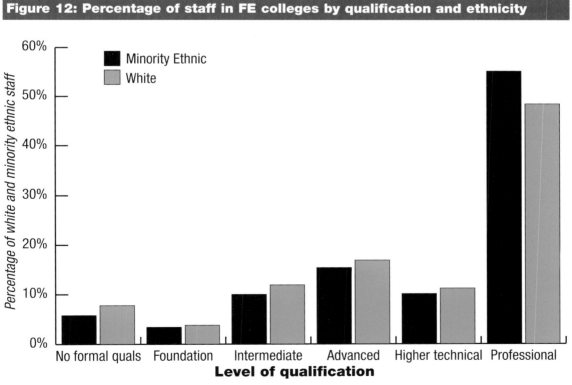

(Source: Staff Individualised Record, LSC, 2000-2001)

Black governors

Research indicates that a significant number of colleges have no Black governors. A survey conducted by e-mail by the Clerks' Network on behalf of the Commission found that 43% of colleges that responded had no Black governors. The survey asked for details about the ethnic mix of college

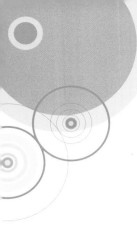
governors and clerks. There were 270 clerks in the network and a total of 134 colleges responded to the survey (including 32 sixth form colleges) from a possible total of 412 colleges in England. The findings showed:

- governors in post   2178
- Black governors   178 (8%)
- Black clerks   1

Figure 13 shows how the proportions of Black governors were distributed in the 134 colleges that responded:

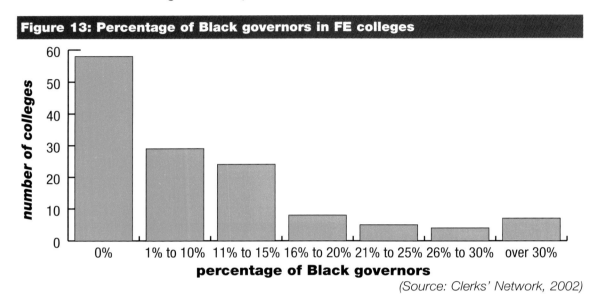

Figure 13: Percentage of Black governors in FE colleges

(Source: Clerks' Network, 2002)

2.4   Black learners

Growth in numbers

Colleges have worked hard to increase the number of learners from minority ethnic groups. The statistics show how successful colleges have been in engaging minority ethnic learners.

Table 14 shows that the percentage of minority ethnic students in further education in England has increased from 12% of the total in 1997-98 to 14% in 1999-2000.[7]

Table 14: Council-funded students in FE by ethnicity			
	1997-98	1998-99	1999-00
Black	4.1%	4.4%	4.4%
Indian	2.2%	2.4%	2.4%
Pakistani/ Bangladeshi	2.7%	2.9%	3.0%
Other Minority	3.1%	3.5%	3.8%
White	87.8%	86.9%	86.4%
Base =	3,251,951	3,113,192	3,029,587
Total	100%	100%	100%

(Source: Individualised Student Record, LSC, 1997-1998, 1998-1999, 1999-2000)

The regional picture

Three regions have particularly high proportions of Black learners. Table 15 illustrates the percentage of minority ethnic students engaged in further education by LSC region. A number of regions have higher proportions of Black students than the 14% national average. In London, the figure is particularly high at 39%, with 15.6% of minority ethnic students in the West Midlands and 12.9% in the East Midlands.

The figures should be seen in the context of findings that show that some groups of minority ethnic young people are more likely to remain in full-time education than their White peers. Four-fifths of all young people from minority ethnic groups have been found to remain in education compared with just over two thirds of White young people.[8] A complete listing of minority ethnic further education student populations by LSC region is provided in appendix D.

Table 15: FE Students 2000-2001 by LSC region and ethnicity

	White	Minority Ethnic	Grand Total	%age Minority Ethnic	%age White
East of England	258,974	26,999	285,973	9.4%	90.6%
East Midlands	242,881	35,981	278,862	12.9%	87.1%
London	330,302	211,582	541,884	39.0%	61.0%
North East	229,509	10,242	239,751	4.3%	95.7%
North West	524,578	47,060	571,638	8.2%	91.8%
South East	418,363	35,358	453,721	7.8%	92.2%
South West	355,324	15,610	370,934	4.2%	95.8%
West Midlands	398,400	73,531	471,931	15.6%	84.4%
Yorkshire & Humberside	320,084	34,823	354,907	9.8%	90.2%
Total	3,078,415	491,186	3,569,601	13.8%	86.2%

(Source: Individualised Student Record, LSC, 2000-2001)

Black learners in predominantly White colleges

LSC data suggests that although the numbers of Black students are rising, many colleges remain mainly White organisations – their leadership and management are predominantly or exclusively from a White European background. Evidence to the Commission from Black staff who felt themselves to be excluded or undervalued raises questions about the experiences of Black students in predominantly White-led organisations and the possible effects of this on retention and achievement.

Black learners in deprived areas

Black learners are more likely than White students to live in areas of social deprivation, which suggests they are more likely to face racism compounded by poverty. Until 1999-2000, only students resident in deprived areas[9] were

eligible for Widening Participation funding. Although the policy was extended to other groups in 1999-2000, the following figures relate only to students living in deprived areas, and show trends in the data over a period of three years. The latest figures (1999-2000) show that the proportion of further education students resident in deprived areas in England as a whole is 27%. The proportion of White further education students living in deprived areas is 22%, whilst the proportions of students from minority ethnic groups are notably higher:

Bangladeshi	76%
Black African	73%
Black Caribbean	67%
Pakistani	68%
Black other	64%

Although proportions of students resident in deprived areas are generally increasing across all ethnic groups, figure 16 provides further illustration of the wide discrepancy between students from minority ethnic groups and their White peers.[10]

Figure 16: Percentage of students living in deprived areas as a proportion of all council-funded students, by ethnicity

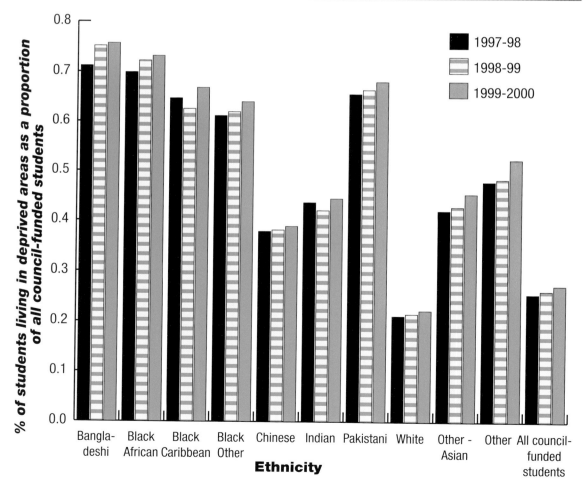

(Source: Individualised Student Record, LSC 1997-1998, 1998-1999, 1999-2000)

Implications for colleges

Many colleges will need to consider the implications of these findings by rethinking their strategies and reviewing and revising policies to reflect the minority ethnic communities they serve. Staff will need a raised understanding of the cultural diversity of their learners. It is incumbent on tutors and learning mentors to take full account of their students' personal and social circumstances to help them learn and achieve. Black learners should be taught by and motivated by both Black and White staff. White students also need to experience positive Black role models, if they are to function properly within a diverse society and the globalised economy.

Achievement of Black learners

Whilst the Commission found no conclusive evidence of a correlation between the low achievement rates of some Black learners and the proportions of Black staff in colleges, there is considerable evidence to suggest that overall Black learners are still underachieving in comparison to their White peers. This is despite an improvement in the levels of achievement for all ethnic groups. The achievement rates in the following table represent the number of students achieving a qualification as a percentage of the total number of students completing courses that lead to a qualification. Table 17 illustrates how minority ethnic students are still underachieving in comparison to their White counterparts, with all minority ethnic groups attaining a lower achievement rate than White students. This is despite a percentage improvement in achievement that is particularly marked for students from minority ethnic groups.[11]

Table 17: Council-funded students in FE: achievements by ethnicity			
Achievement rate by ethnicity	1997-98	1998-99	%age change
Bangladeshi	61.5%	64.8%	3.3%
Black African	54.6%	61.0%	6.4%
Black Caribbean	57.3%	62.0%	4.7%
Black Other	59.9%	63.4%	3.5%
Chinese	62.0%	67.7%	5.7%
Indian	63.2%	68.9%	5.7%
Pakistani	59.6%	64.2%	4.6%
White	71.8%	72.0%	0.2%
Other - Asian	60.8%	67.4%	6.6%
Other	59.8%	66.0%	6.2%
All students	70.2%	71.0%	0.8%

* Students with unknown ethnicities are excluded from this analysis
(Source: Individualised Student Record, LSC, 1997-1998, 1998-1999, 1999-2000)

Further research is needed to establish whether there is a correlation between the low achievement rate of Black learners and the proportion of Black staff in colleges.

2.5 Conclusions

The Commission's findings provide some key indicators for assessing the position of Black staff and students in the sector compared with their position in the general population. It is evident that Black staff are under-represented generally within colleges throughout England. This under-representation takes on a much greater significance when Black staffing levels are compared with specific regional and local areas with high numbers of Black people in the population. The disparity is also evident when comparing Black staff and Black learners in many colleges.

An analysis of staffing roles also indicates that there is under-representation of Black staff at management and senior management level. The situation is compounded by Black staff being more likely to be on fixed term contracts and employed in part-time hourly paid teaching positions. This situation cannot be explained by reference to the level of qualifications held by Black staff, which shows they are more likely to have a qualification compared with White staff and to be educated to a higher level overall.

The employment position of Black staff highlights disparities which have clear implications for colleges in their efforts to eliminate unlawful discrimination and promote race equality. It also raises questions about the possible impact on the retention and achievement of Black learners, who need positive role models they can emulate at all levels of the college hierarchy.

More detailed findings from the Commission's research are set out in chapter 5.

Notes

1. All statistics presented in the following pages use the term 'minority ethnic' to refer to visible minority groups.

2. Office for National Statistics, *Regional trends 36 – 2001 Edition* at: http://www.statistics.gov.uk/statbase, using data from the Labour Force Survey.

3. Unitary Authority and Local Authority Districts (UALADs) data are provided by the Office for National Statistics from the *Labour Force Survey* (Winter 2000-01). The London borough data form a sub-set of the UALADs data. Some of the figures provided are below the ONS threshold level and are therefore unreliable.

   The data are not directly comparable with *Labour Force Survey* data taken from *Regional trends 36 – 2001* Edition for the following reasons: i) they are from a single quarter (Winter 2000-01), whereas the regional trends data are taken from four quarters (Spring 2000 to Winter 2001) and then averaged; and ii) the datasets are based on different ethnic classifications.

4. Further education staff data are provided by the Learning and Skills Council from the *Staff Individualised Record 9* (2000-01). The statistics used here are based on SIR data for staff who work at least 25% of a full-time job, giving a total of 218,107 members of staff throughout England. Thirteen per cent of this total are excluded because no data are available for ethnicity, leaving a total of 189,094 used in analysis.

5. Figure 5 shows that both in the South West and the South East, the rates for staff and population are the same (4% in the South East and 2% in the South West).

6. These data are provided by the Learning and Skills Council from the *Staff Individualised Record 9 (2000-01).* Data for 74% (162, 221) of the original 218,107 members of staff provide the necessary information on both ethnicity and qualifications to be used in the analysis.

7. Learning and Skills Council, *Widening participation in further education – statistical evidence 1999-2000* at: http://www.lscdata.gov.uk/data/statistical_evidence.html

8. Owen, D et al (2000) *Minority Ethnic Participation and Achievements in Education, Training and the Labour Market* Research Brief, DfEE, using data from Youth Cohort Study 9 sweep 1, 1998.

9. Areas of deprivation are based on the DETR Indices of Deprivation 2000 at: www.urban.odpm/research/id2000/index.htm. The index is based on the premise that a measure of deprivation can be made up from the following dimensions (or domains): income; employment; health deprivation and disability; education, skills and training; housing; and geographical access to services.

10. Learning and Skills Council, op. cit.

11. Learning and Skills Council, op. cit.

Chapter 3

Black staff in further education: the qualitative evidence

3.1   Key findings

The witness evidence heard by the Commission suggests that:

- Black staff in inclusive colleges feel valued, motivated and able to achieve their professional ambitions

- many colleges do not acknowledge racism as an issue or know how to tackle it effectively

- there are few senior Black managers to act as role models for Black and White staff and for learners

- a 'glass ceiling' has prevented Black staff progressing into management, and into permanent posts from temporary or part-time posts

- the qualifications, experience and contributions of Black staff are generally under-valued

- restructuring, mergers and other organisational changes have resulted in discriminatory practices and the erosion of good equalities practice

- a significant number of Black staff feel marginalised, bullied and unsupported, or involved in college functions and activities in a tokenistic way

- trade unions have not always tackled racism effectively

- managers need training to increase their confidence in dealing with racism

- all staff, both Black and White, require training in equality and diversity issues

- more Black staff will be needed as colleges continue to widen participation and the number of Black learners increases.

3.2   The witness days

The evidence presented in this chapter represents an authentic voice from within the sector. During ten witness days held at colleges around the UK during 2000 and 2001, some 200 individuals, both Black and White, spoke of their personal experiences of institutional racism in colleges. Their testimonies convey something of the challenges of working in further education in multicultural Britain in the 21st century. (See appendix A.)

The witness evidence provides a unique perspective on the issues that concern the Commission. Many of the themes identified help to substantiate the quantitative evidence already outlined. However subjective, the comments and perceptions outlined here warrant the sector's scrutiny. They offer some invaluable insights into the day-to-day lives of Black staff and suggest actions that colleges could take to change organisational culture.

The evidence, once transcribed, comprised several hundred pages and it is impossible to do justice to the full range of views and experiences conveyed. It was not the task of the Commission to investigate or take up the individual issues raised, or to test the veracity of the evidence. Its task was to report the evidence as faithfully as possible and to highlight the key issues by summarising the most common areas of concern. The quotes in this section

and throughout the report are from staff who participated in the witness day events. They include college principals, senior and middle managers, union officials, support staff, lecturers and part-time tutors. Because of the sensitive nature of the evidence given, considerable care has been taken to protect the identity of both the individuals and organisations involved.

3.3   The evidence

Equalities infrastructure

'Policies appear to exist on paper, but are not working in practice. You can put anything on paper, but it doesn't mean you will see a difference.'

'There are very high demands on senior Black staff to be involved in all equal opportunities work, including staff support, dealing with complaints or problem students and managing their normal workload. In this sense, they are being set up to fail.'

Institutional commitment

A number of staff, both Black and White, referred to the ineffectiveness of their college's equality policies or questioned the extent of institutional commitment to them. Their concerns focused on areas such as:

- inappropriate or ineffective leadership and race equality 'champions' with responsibility for mainstreaming and co-ordinating race and equality
- the lack of clear codes of practice to support policy implementation
- the inappropriate or ineffective equality committee structures, often with no Black representation
- the lack of access to or limited circulation of equality-related documentation
- the lack of cross-college representation, or people being appointed to sit on equality committees because of their position rather than their expertise
- the uneven application of equality policies and procedures particularly in relation to grievances and performance appraisal[1]
- the lack of consultation with Black staff in the development and implementation of race and equality policies.

Leadership and management

'Black senior managers in the college are represented in higher proportions than they appear in the local population and within the college community. We have a monthly data analysis of HR performance, staff recruitment and

*disciplinaries and management meetings to devise
actions to address any inequalities.'*

*'It's an absolutely necessary condition of any success that as the
head of the organisation I keep on and on without letting up.'*

The role of governors, principals and senior managers in actively
'championing' and promoting policies is widely acknowledged and their
accountability is a central theme in the leadership and management strand of
the revised common inspection framework. Many witnesses claimed that
Black staff felt under pressure to take responsibility for promoting race equality
issues. They stressed that it was vital to develop equality policies collectively,
involving all staff as well as consulting with trade unions to encourage cross-
college ownership.

Evidence from the Inland Revenue stressed the absolute necessity of clear
and firm leadership in achieving change on race and equalities. Leadership
was seen to begin with raising awareness so that everyone understood what
valuing diversity meant and how it enhanced what they did.

Equalities policies

Data from the national survey suggested that most colleges had equal
opportunity policies in place, although prior to 31st May 2002 very few had a
specific policy on race equality. The survey also revealed variations in the way
colleges developed and enforced their equality practices and procedures. It
also suggested that Black staff were less likely than their White colleagues to
regard their institution's equality policies as effective.

Ethnic monitoring

*'Colleges should be using their internal data to benchmark their
own performance. If the population of Black students is 50%,
then questions should be asked about why the staff are not
Black at all levels. There should also be some analysis of staff
qualifications and experience and the findings used to develop
best practice and set targets. This sort of analysis should also
be applied when looking at student performance and looking
for any disparities in achievement across ethnic groups.'*

*'If I receive an application without the data I need for
monitoring purposes, I send it back to them with a polite
letter saying that although this isn't a legal requirement, it is
very useful for the college to have this information. The letter
explains that we need it so that we can make sure we do not
discriminate against anyone because of their race, gender or
disability. Most people fill it in and return it. If they refuse, it's
a clear signal to me that this person probably doesn't
understand the equalities agenda.'*

The availability of accurate and accessible data was viewed as essential to systematic ethnic monitoring, yet the difficulties of gaining access to ethnic data, particularly the ethnic profile of staff, were widely acknowledged. The development of mandatory targets covering all the relevant college functions was considered essential if colleges were to effect real change. The Race Relations (Amendment) Act now requires all colleges to develop effective monitoring systems and transparent reporting procedures.

Positive role models

'Colleges often have pictures of senior management teams and governors in their reception. These send out messages. They are the role models offered for others to emulate.'

The lack of high profile Black and Asian role models was a key theme throughout the witness evidence. This situation with regard to the political process has been described by the current Prime Minister as 'not a record of pride'.[2] Bill Morris, general secretary of the Transport and General Workers' Union, when commenting on the fact that only 2% of MPs were from African, Caribbean or Asian communities, argued that minority ethnic groups would have little reason to engage with the political process if they could not identify with the politicians that represented them.[3] The same message is true for Black learners and potential job applicants who all need to identify colleges as safe, welcoming and inclusive.

Promoting positive images of diversity through positive Black role models, particularly at senior management level, was seen as vital if colleges were to encourage more Black staff into the sector. Black role models at all levels within the college hierarchy were also seen as essential for Black learners who needed access to role models and mentors in positions of power and influence who could 'illustrate professional potential'. The benefits to White learners were also highlighted, particularly in predominantly White areas.

Promoting diversity

Witnesses expressed the view that colleges should be more welcoming of diversity by promoting a multicultural, inclusive ethos, regardless of the ethnic profile of their staff, students or local community. This was seen as imperative for colleges with a public commitment to inclusive learning and widening participation. More welcoming messages, positive visual images and increasingly prominent Black role models were needed.

In one college, with a large multicultural population of learners, examples of promoting diversity included a multicultural fashion show, positive and diverse images of learners, multi-faith prayer rooms and catering facilities with a varied menu catering for a range of dietary requirements. Staff regarded the availability of diverse social facilities for learners as a means of developing and spreading good practice. They emphasised the development of anti-racist curricula and policies for learners and the value of opportunities provided to work with like-minded groups in schools.

Recruitment and selection

'There is a reasonable number of Black staff in lower levels of the organisation, but only a handful in senior and course management positions.'

Inappropriate recruitment and selection practices and their impact on opportunities for progression were major themes of the Commission's inquiry. Witnesses' concerns focused on:

- the circumvention of established procedures, particularly when appointing part-time or hourly paid teaching staff
- racially biased recruitment and selection practices, particularly at times of merger or restructuring or when seconding or redeploying staff
- the undervaluing of relevant experience and of overseas or non-traditional qualifications
- 'tokenism', particularly on internal committees and interview panels
- the 'glass ceiling' and its negative effect on progression and retention
- extended or over-use of temporary and part-time contracts
- the 'ghettoisation' of Black staff in certain subject areas[4]
- inconsistent or ineffective use of ethnic monitoring and data collection.

Many of these issues were also highlighted by research commissioned by the Learning and Skills Development Agency[5]. Some key points are set out in appendix E.

Recruitment and selection procedures

Racial bias in recruitment and selection was seen by witnesses to have a negative impact on both external and internal appointments. In some instances, college recruitment and selection procedures or protocols were said to have been openly ignored or circumvented. Concerns were also voiced about the lack of transparency in appointment and decision-making processes.

Black managers who gave evidence felt particularly affected by restructuring and redundancies. One witness described how senior posts previously occupied by White colleagues had been downgraded before being reassigned to Black managers. There was also a perception that Black managers were expected to do more than their White counterparts in return for lower status and pay.

Part-time appointments

'Often key posts are already identified for particular people through ring fencing. People are encouraged and appointed according to whether their face fits.'

The appointment of part-time, hourly paid teaching staff was seen as especially problematic. The national survey found that under half (42%) of all

institutions surveyed used formal recruitment procedures when appointing part-time staff. Despite numerical evidence that Black staff were more likely to be employed on temporary or part-time contracts, informal recruitment practices were still felt to be particularly discriminatory. Often serving as a 'first rung' into permanent employment, many Black staff felt strongly that their access to permanent employment in colleges was curtailed by the informal recruitment practices of White colleagues.

Informal recruitment practices

'Internal posts at management level are not subject to the college's own recruitment and selection procedures. Most appointments are based on cronyism and not merit or ability.'

Some witnesses reported that informal recruitment practices were seen to stem from a 'pub and barbecue culture' or an over-reliance on exclusive social networks which disadvantaged potential Black recruits, particularly those from non-Christian and asylum-seeking communities.

Internally advertised posts, including secondments, were also seen by some staff as particularly open to informal recruitment practices, even at managerial level. Several witnesses spoke of procedures or protocols that had been ignored or openly circumvented.

Progression

Good practice

The Commission heard several encouraging examples of good practice. For example the support, trust and responsibility afforded by one White senior manager was described as empowering by one witness, who was in no doubt that her job had been awarded on merit. She had experienced no problems and felt accepted by her White colleagues. Another witness had moved quickly into a senior management position and was confident of realising her ambitions to become a principal by the time she was 40.

Barriers to progression

In contrast, many witnesses regarded progression from middle to senior management positions as especially difficult, with the 'glass ceiling' acting as a severe restriction[6] particularly in colleges where staff turnover was low. In many cases, it was reported that interviews for key senior management posts were conducted by governors who had received little or no training in equalities issues and had little understanding of the negative impact of stereotypes on recruitment and selection processes. There were similar concerns about the lack of equalities training for other staff in interviewing or personnel roles. Lack of training was also raised as an issue by Black staff deployed on interviewing panels.

However some evidence demonstrated that there were also pro-active governors in the sector who were determined to take action to address race equality:

'Following a race and sex discrimination grievance brought against the college, governors were concerned about perceptions of more generalised racism and sexism. We asked the principal to draw up a schedule of action points to address them. Part of the action plan involved seeking the views of Black workers. A number of suggestions were put forward to remedy the situation. They included ensuring that all staff development opportunities had an equal opportunities perspective and provided training that focused on managing conflict, raising staff confidence to deal with conflict or contentious issues and raising awareness of prejudice and perceptions.'

Qualifications and experience

Witnesses acknowledged that many colleges were committed to widening participation and valued the role of Black staff in attracting or supporting Black learners. However some witnesses stressed that they felt that this experience was under-valued in the context of career progression and promotion. There was also a view that qualifications gained overseas or at 'new' universities were more likely to be overlooked or ignored during shortlisting and interviews.

'Tokenism'

The use of Black staff as a form of organisational 'window-dressing', leaving them without access to positions of genuine influence, was identified as 'tokenism'. Witnesses gave several examples, including:

- the use of untrained Black staff on interview panels in order to present a favourable image of the institution to potential applicants

- the promotion of individuals 'because of the colour of their skin and their cultural links' rather than on merit

- the use of isolated, powerless or unrepresentative individuals on college committees, in order to claim Black representation.

Improving retention

'There is a culture of secrecy and exclusion that makes dedicated staff feel isolated, devalued and marginalised.'

For some witnesses, more effective support systems for tackling marginalisation were seen as a high priority for colleges wishing to retain Black learners and staff, particularly in mainly White areas. Their evidence focused on:

- the challenges of working or learning in predominantly White colleges, often in isolation or with little managerial support

- unrepresentative governing bodies and decision-making structures

- the lack of support for staff who encountered racism

- bullying and harassment, including pressure to conform.

Mentoring

Available research suggests that mentoring and coaching schemes are among the most effective mechanisms for developing and retaining staff. Research into the career progression of minorities in US corporations[7] found distinct patterns in the career advancement of White employees and minorities, with White professionals tending to progress much earlier in their careers. However a significant factor in the career advancement of 'people of colour' was their access to 'a strong network of mentors and corporate sponsors who nurture their professional development'. Evidence to the Commission strongly supports the development of a targeted national Black mentoring programme to help tackle under-representation, particularly at senior management level.

Stereotyping

'Students and staff at the college are often surprised when they find out I'm a lecturer. As a Black woman, students expect me to be the office receptionist, canteen lady or secretary.'

Racial stereotypes

Racial stereotyping by students, colleagues or managers was cited as a key concern by several witnesses, and was seen as a direct influence both in and outside the classroom. Assumptions, claimed witnesses, were made about:

- the competence or behaviour patterns of Black staff or learners
- the jobs they could best carry out or were most likely to be in
- their authority, status or qualifications.

Racial stereotypes were expressed in different ways. Several witnesses reported that they had experienced hostility, harassment or verbal abuse. Others had experiences of being challenged by caretakers, receptionists or colleagues in 'gatekeeper' roles who had questioned their presence or authority, often in an embarrassing or confrontational way.

Low expectations

'My manager explained the task to me really slowly on more than one occasion, as if he thought I was stupid.'

'I no longer apply for promotions because I'm not encouraged to. I've never got any of the jobs I've applied for despite being the most qualified and experienced person in my team.'

Available research suggests that low expectations can lead to a 'self-fulfilling prophecy' with individuals internalising and in some cases 'acting out' what is expected of them. Both the Rampton Report[8] and Swann Report[9] highlighted the effects of low teacher expectations on African-Caribbean children in schools. The low expectations of colleagues and managers are likely to have similarly demotivating effects on adults, reinforcing barriers or feelings of exclusion. Both Black and White witnesses referred to the stereotypical assumptions of White learners, which could lead them to question the authority or competence of Black staff, especially those in teaching or managerial roles.

Assumptions about Black learners

The impact of negative attitudes on student retention and attainment warrants more detailed research. Stereotyping was thought by some witnesses to have a damaging effect on students, particularly African-Caribbean and Asian boys who were most likely to be typecast as aggressive or confrontational. This was highlighted by the evidence of a group of Black learners, who spoke eloquently of the 'rude and disrespectful' behaviour of some security guards; and of the negative perceptions of some staff, particularly towards learners whose first language was not English. Some felt that the teaching and support they received was less effective due to some tutors' low expectations.

Assumptions by learners

'I have sometimes found it difficult teaching classes of totally White students. They have no concept of what racism is and constantly question my position and authority.'

'The students in my college have a less than equal perception of Black staff and they don't perceive Black staff in programme leader roles. They identify with White staff and prefer to go to them for information.'

A number of witnesses spoke of the difficulties of Black lecturers working in predominantly White colleges, stressing the need to challenge the attitudes of White learners who are disrespectful to Black lecturing staff or dismissive of race issues. In colleges with large numbers of Black learners, equally undermining attitudes were sometimes expressed by individual Black students who perceive urban colleges with Black staff and large concentrations of minority ethnic students as second-class provision.

Bullying and harassment

'After only a few weeks at the college, I began to experience racist innuendo and horseplay. Over four years there were some 40 incidents, including people urinating in my coffee and threats of physical violence.'

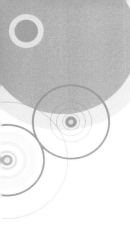

'Black staff are very used to racial comments from White colleagues. There seems to be an acceptance of this practice by senior management because even when people are challenged about their behaviour, nothing appears to be done. The college operates an "old boys network" and incidents just seem to get covered up.'

There were recurring stories of harassment and bullying received throughout the Commission's inquiry. Black staff who had complained about or tried to challenge racism generally or racist incidents reported that they had found themselves ignored or stereotyped as 'trouble-makers'. The Commission heard examples of staff who felt isolated, bullied or harassed by learners, individual colleagues, line managers or by members of their senior management team. Many of the allegations of bullying and harassment related to:

- negative views about the competence of Black staff, sometimes leading to an over-critical or over-controlling management style

- a disproportionately heavy or difficult workload

- suspicion and mistrust

- Black staff feeling under constant pressure to prove themselves

- Black staff in positions that lacked appropriate support or offered no staff development opportunities

- feeling undermined or not taken seriously

- feeling under constant pressure to prove themselves

- complaints by learners which were thought to have been instigated by managers or colleagues.

(See definition of harassment in the glossary.)

Management styles

The case study research found that poor or bullying management styles were a factor in colleges' failure to retain their staff. Numerous examples of bullying and other inappropriate treatment were provided in the witness evidence. A tutor, for example, told the Commission she had been instructed to deliver 11 units of a course single-handedly, due to staff sickness on her team, despite having alerted managers to ongoing racial abuse by the mainly White, working-class learners. Other accounts centred on:

- veiled threats from line managers

- insults and verbal abuse

- being treated as a novice

- feeling undermined or over-controlled.

Support

The issue of support was seen by a number of witnesses as an aggravating factor in their experience of bullying behaviour. Some witnesses reported that bullying was most likely to be experienced in predominantly White institutions that lacked an effective race and equalities infrastructure. Others described working in marginal positions in colleges with little support. Stereotyping was considered to be at the root of criticism about the competence of Black staff, although some witnesses felt they had been typecast as 'tough and therefore not needing support'. Many Black staff spoke of feeling unsupported and isolated, particularly when they first started a job or gained promotion. In the absence of formal induction and mentoring programmes, several had relied on individual colleagues, informal 'buddies' or friendship networks for support.

The net effect of harassment on some individuals had been poor health, resulting in high levels of absence, depression, low morale, loss of confidence and poor work performance.

A number of colleges have acknowledged the need for more effective support by setting up focus groups, mentoring or buddying schemes. Others have sought to reduce the incidence of harassment by identifying and training equalities representatives in different departments or sites, who could be approached in confidence for informal advice and support.

Acknowledging the problem

'Senior managers seem to be either in denial ... or frightened of staff feeling threatened by their attempts to deal with the issue ... consequently, management seems to be very defensive about any mention of racism and the issue is not discussed in any meaningful way.'

A number of witnesses described situations where Black staff have had to raise issues individually. This placed an unfair responsibility on those prepared to 'raise their heads above the parapet'. Others felt they had been victimised, scapegoated or challenged for their attempts to put racism on the college agenda. It was felt that more open debate was needed about institutional racism and that staff focus groups presented an appropriate forum for safe dialogue and consultation, enabling Black staff to voice their concerns and suggestions collectively.

Complaints and grievances

Grievance procedures

Some Black staff felt a strong sense of injustice about complaints of racism. They felt these complaints had been ignored or not treated seriously and that grievance procedures were inadequate for dealing with race issues, particularly in the early stages of a grievance when there was frequently no other Black person to talk to. This had led to staff feeling alienated and more inclined to seek legal advice from a solicitor. Some of the concerns raised included:

- complaints being ignored, dismissed or treated more seriously when they came from students

- attempts to dissuade individuals from complaining

- complaints not being investigated within a reasonable period

- a lack of follow-up, including feedback to complainants and line managers

- managers lacking the confidence to deal with racist incidents

- a lack of transparent investigative procedures

- the absence of a forum to raise concerns or seek support

- colleagues perceiving Black people as 'strong' and therefore not in need of support

- complaints about being labelled as 'trouble-makers'

- people making a complaint of racism experiencing victimisation and marginalisation, which could lead to a transfer as a result (see glossary for definition of victimisation)

- Black staff being afraid to complain about racist incidents for fear of losing their job

- incidence of stress-related sick leave due to experiences of racism at work

- 'gagging' or confidentiality clauses in tribunal cases helping to mask the extent of racism in colleges, thereby discouraging any learning by the organisation.

Union attitudes

Concerns about attitudes within trade unions at branch level were raised by witnesses. It was thought such attitudes had discouraged some Black staff from joining their union or playing a more active role. Some witnesses said lay officers and full-time officials were reluctant to acknowledge or pursue grievances where racism was a factor. Some described situations where their complaints had not been taken seriously, with explanations such as 'a personality conflict' used to rationalise the racist behaviour of managers or colleagues. Consequently, Black members were more likely to seek redress through solicitors. A number of witnesses described their experiences of seeking union support as negative:

'As well as the pressure from senior managers and the threatening atmosphere within the college, I also had to contend with the failure of my union to support me and what experienced as the union's active collusion with college management. When I first approached my union, they refused to take up my case. Eventually I found a sympathetic union rep, who passed on details of my case to a regional officer. I was then able to pursue my case in a tribunal.'

'I tried in vain to raise my concerns about bullying and institutional racism in meetings with my union rep. He was dismissive, defensive and seemed only prepared to take up my case if it had involved explicit racist name-calling. He seemed to have no concept of institutional racism.'

Members' perceptions

There was a view of unions as predominantly White organisations with few Black officers or officials. This had led to a perception amongst many Black staff, both members and non-members, that unions did not always:

- understand racism and cultural diversity and how this impacted upon individuals

- vigorously pursue complaints of racial discrimination and other matters affecting Black staff

- challenge racism within unions themselves

- support Black staff whose jobs were threatened by mergers or restructuring

- support Black members in taking out a grievance or going to tribunal on the grounds of racism

- give appropriate advice and support to members who were involved in a grievance or tribunal case concerning race discrimination.

This view of unions must be seen in the context of evidence that race discrimination tribunal cases have a much lower chance of success than other tribunal cases[10] and that 'tribunals have been unable or unwilling to offer the same recourse for those alleging race discrimination as for those making other types of claims.'[11]

Successful union interventions

'The only support I've received throughout is from some union officers. They are working flat out to try and monitor bad practices at the college, with a view to eradicating the climate of cronyism, racism, sexual harassment and bullying.'

By way of contrast, the Commission also heard some strong statements about the support received by Black staff from their unions. In one case, a Black staff group had been established as a direct result of trade union intervention, enabling group members to raise issues collectively with college management. One union in particular was described as having 'a strong and sincere position relating to equality and discrimination.'

Restructuring

'The merger left the college dominated by a White management.'

Some Black staff felt they had been affected disproportionately by college redundancy and restructuring processes. A number of witnesses believed these had not been undertaken fairly and impartially. The issues raised about restructuring included:

- poor communication with staff

- the erosion of good equalities practice

- the downgrading of posts most likely to be held by Black staff

- the adverse impact on career progression

- shifts in the culture of the organisation which led to the marginalisation of Black staff

- the downgrading of equality issues

- the closure of targeted or low-earning courses and the potentially negative impact on access to mainstream provision by Black learners or local communities.

Erosion of good practice

A number of witnesses believed that good equalities practice had been eroded because of college merger or restructuring activities. One described how 15 years of developing good practice, including training for staff, and the use of union representatives on interview panels had been 'dumped'. Similar concerns that equalities issues had been put on the bottom of the college agenda as a result of incorporation were highlighted in a report by Farish et al in 1995.[12] Evidence from witnesses echoes concerns about restructuring in local authorities. Equal opportunities, targeting and monitoring activities are described as having 'fallen by the board' in a number of London boroughs in the late 1990s, with large numbers of Black staff sacked in a process of retrenchment.[13] Further research is needed into the impact of restructuring on specific groups within the sector. However it is a requirement under the Race Relations (Amendment) Act for those leading college mergers to explore the race equality implications and to monitor the impact. There is also, clearly, an important role for unions in the early stages of any restructuring activity in keeping equalities issues high on the college's agenda.

Black staff focus groups

'The role of our forum is to help Black and ethnic minority staff support the college in tackling institutional racism; to improve employment training and job prospects for Black staff; and to ensure that services are appropriate and represent the interests of Black staff and learners. The forum contributes to the college's newsletter and to working parties or sub-committees that look at existing policies or suggest new ones.'

Black staff focus groups, networks or forums were thought to be important tools for voicing concerns about racism and for sharing information, support and experiences. However, it was felt that such groups could only be effective if they were:

- actively supported by college senior managers, with financial assistance and time off to attend meetings

- guided by clear terms of reference

- effectively led and administered
- part of the college's consultation infrastructure
- afforded specific roles – for example reviewing college policies or ethnic data
- able to operate without undue managerial control or influence
- able to debate issues that might be perceived by others as negative or too challenging
- given explicit mechanisms for feeding views and suggestions through to relevant committees and decision-makers.

There was a view that Black support groups could be seen as threatening or divisive or had proven ineffective, particularly when their efforts had been undermined by line managers or complaints by White colleagues about 'special treatment'. Some Black staff saw attempts to form such groups as a management 'window dressing exercise' that could not genuinely represent the views of Black staff; or they were afraid to attend for fear of being labelled. This was thought to be the main cause of poor attendance in some colleges.

Staff training and development

'As a trainer, I have often encountered individuals who have been damaged by past experiences of race awareness training. They tend to be more defensive about bad practice or less receptive to key training messages. It takes a lot of skill to break down these barriers and the facilitator needs considerable patience and experience to achieve that kind of breakthrough, especially if they've only been given half a day or a day.'

'It is often maintained that Black staff need training to bring them up to the standard of their White colleagues or that Black staff have been denied access to training, but Black people applying for jobs often have superior qualifications and experience yet still they don't get appointed.'

Staff training needs

Witnesses identified three broad areas to be addressed in order to meet staff training and development needs:

- more equalities training, including targeted or mandatory training for different groups of staff
- specific training for all staff on how to tackle discrimination, promote good race relations and handle racist incidents
- access by Black staff to staff development opportunities and to targeted or fast-track training.

Equality and diversity training

Witnesses felt that all staff were entitled to training in equality and diversity issues to ensure that they:

- did not discriminate intentionally or unwittingly
- were able to comply with the law
- were effective in implementing race and equality policies.

There were concerns that the lack of appropriate training for staff at all levels, including governors and senior managers, helped reinforce discriminatory practices. Staff could not be expected to manage the new race and equalities agenda without effective training and support. Equalities training for governors was seen as a particular priority if they were to oversee and monitor the implementation of college race and equality policies.

Staff resistance

There was a belief that some staff in colleges were overtly racist and unwilling to change, resulting in low attendance or resistance to key training messages. Others were seen as complacent or unaware of how their individual behaviour helped to reinforce institutional racism. Some witnesses felt that senior managers often found it difficult to understand how racism operated and how to deal with it effectively, yet failed to see their own training needs as a priority. A number of witnesses acknowledged:

- the need for staff development in best practice in race equality to be of the highest standard and to include Black trainers where possible
- the need for appropriate and relevant training materials such as clearer guidance on the distinction between positive action and positive discrimination
- the need to ensure that training empowered staff to teach all learners about racism and other equalities issues – this would increase learners' awareness of how racism operated both at an institutional and a personal level.

Specific or targeted training

The view was that materials and specialist training needed to be targeted at different groups of staff. For example, Black staff in multi-ethnic colleges might need to focus on particular empowerment issues or training needs identified in focus group discussions. However, training targeted at different ethnic groups could be seen as divisive, and needed to be carefully explained and promoted to ensure that staff understood the need for such an approach.

Training for Black staff

Lack of training alone did not explain the under-representation of Black staff within the sector or their lack of progression, once employed. Nevertheless, witnesses raised several issues relating to the training needs of Black staff. Their views echoed those of many White colleagues and related to:

- the lack of formal induction, particularly of part-time staff

- the difficulties faced by support staff wishing to attend training, where cover had not been arranged

- requests to take on extra responsibilities, without receiving appropriate training or recognition

- the need for more training for potential and actual managers

- the need for more opportunities to shadow managers and access work experience opportunities where they could develop and practice new skills

- the need for more opportunities to undertake higher education, teacher training or postgraduate courses.

Training on handling racist incidents

The evidence from witnesses suggested that racist name-calling, harassment and stereotyping remained commonplace in some colleges, yet both Black and White staff seemed unsure about how to deal with racist incidents. The evidence suggested that many colleges had no effective policies or planned training in this area. In some cases, the prevailing culture in colleges was thought to be permissive, with managers 'opting for a quiet life' by not challenging or penalising the perpetrators. One witness claimed that she had resigned and chosen to teach in the private sector because 'a culture of racism' had been allowed to continue unchecked. There is anecdotal evidence to suggest that Islamaphobia and the number of racially motivated attacks have increased post-11th September, confirming that much more thought needs to be given by colleges about how to actively discourage such incidents.

Meeting learners' needs

'The college draws students from all over the world and is one of the most diverse places you will find anywhere. That diversity is one of our greatest assets – we are proud of it, and believe that it will enrich your experience here. We are just as passionate about equality of opportunity and are working to create a college where everyone has a chance to learn and work, free from discrimination, prejudice or fear.'

Although Black staff are the key focus of the Commission's inquiry, one of its strategic aims is to 'raise the achievement level of all who work and learn in further education'. A major theme running throughout the witness day events was the negative impact on Black learners resulting from the under-representation of Black staff and the failure of colleges to tackle institutional racism more effectively.

Concerns were voiced by both Black and White witnesses in a range of roles who drew attention to:

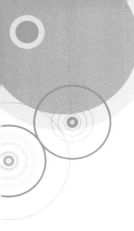

The curriculum:

'Despite the fact that the students are predominantly Asian the syllabus does not reflect this, for example, in music technology, they study mostly European music.'

Among the key strategies for meeting Black learners' needs and tackling under-achievement was the development of curricula that draw from a range of cultures, continents, backgrounds and experiences.

Role models:

'Students have very few Black role models. Staffing in the college does not reflect the student make up, yet the college is claiming additional money for working with Black students.'

Tackling the under-representation of Black and other identified groups of staff would provide learners with a greater diversity of role-models. Witnesses felt that funding should be targeted to benefit learners directly.

Exclusions:

At one college, *'there had been 30 exclusions, 26 of whom were Black students. The reasons given were not consistent and appeared to take a stereotypical view of students.'*

Stereotypes were perceived as playing an important part in the attitudes of staff towards particular groups of students, leading to unfounded fears, low expectations and confrontational attitudes. Colleges with high exclusion rates had benefited from explicit and well-negotiated behavioural codes for both staff and learners, combined with sensitive staff training on how to handle inappropriate or potentially threatening behaviour.

Cultural diversity:

'Muslim staff and parents emphasised the need for a separate common room for girls at the college, as well as for a prayer room for staff and students. Food to meet the specific cultural and religious dietary requirements of our community is still not provided by the college. There are no signs or posters in community languages.'

'The college serves a diverse community and is committed to eliminating discrimination and promoting equality of opportunity. It is essential, therefore, that all contractors support and reinforce the college's policies in this area and

understand the need to take them into full account when designing and delivering services'.

The need for colleges to respond to the increasing cultural and social diversity of learners was a common theme. It was evident from the Commission's research that many colleges have made considerable strides towards meeting the needs of Black learners. Among the key strategies was ensuring that contracted organisations were fully aware of and committed to promoting race equality when providing catering, security and other services to colleges. This was spelt out clearly in a contract specification shared with the Commission.

Other issues raised related to:

- the need for colleges with many Black learners to attract more teachers who have an awareness of cultural diversity, an understanding of learners' needs and a knowledge of race and equality issues

- the tendency to equate the dialect and accent of some Black learners with literacy or English language needs

- the failure of some colleges to address the particular learning and support needs of asylum-seekers

- disparities between the college income attracted by Black learners and the resources made available to meet their learning needs

Individual witnesses and key stakeholder organisations stressed that the current under-achievement of Black learners needs to be tackled urgently. It is also important to establish what links there may be between low achievement rates of learners and the under-representation of Black staff in colleges.

It is the view of the Commission that the problems highlighted by the qualitative evidence in this report provide important complementary data to the quantitative evidence. These issues need to be properly explored and rapidly addressed by colleges and other key agencies.

Notes

1.   Studies of appraisal performance in the civil service have shown that White staff were awarded higher marks than non-White staff at each grade. A link was established between performance and job satisfaction. Commission for Racial Equality (2001) *Ethnic monitoring: A guide for public authorities.*

2.   Rushanara and O' Cinneide (2002) *Our house? Race and representation in British Politics,* London: Institute for Public Policy Research, p.1.

3.   *The Observer* (2002) 28 April.

4.   The University of North London survey found a disproportionate number of Black lecturers employed in continuing education, including basic skills and English for Speakers of Other Languages.

5.   Learning and Skills Development Agency and the Commission for Black Staff in Further Education (April 2002) *Black issues in recruitment procedures and processes in the further education sector.*

6.   Carter J, Fenton, S and Modood, T (1999) *Ethnicity and Employment in Higher Education,* London: Policy Studies Institute.

7.   David Thomas, The truth about mentoring minorities: Race matters, in *Harvard Business Review* (April 2001), p. 99.

8.   Rampton, A (1981) *West Indian Children in our Schools: Interim Report of the Committee of Inquiry into the Education of Children from Ethnic Minority Groups,* Series: Cmnd., 8273, London: HMSO.

9.   Swann, M, B (1985) *Education for All: The Report of the Committee of Enquiry into the Education of Children from Ethnic Minority Groups,* presented to Parliament by the Secretary for Education and Science Series: Cmnd. 9453, London: HMSO.

10. **WHAT JUSTICE?**

Success rate at tribunal hearings (2000-2001)

Redundancy	65%
Wages Act cases	60%
Working time	56%
Breach of contract	49%
Unfair dismissal	31%
Sex discrimination	28%
Disability discrimination	20%
Race discrimination	16%
All jurisdictions	43%

(Labour Research, 2002:15)

11. A survey in 1992, carried out by Labour Research, found that race discrimination cases had the highest withdrawal rate without any form of settlement, of any type of claim. This situation has changed very little in the intervening years. Labour Research Department (2002) *Labour Research.*

12. Farish, M, McPake, J, Powney, J and Weiner, G (1995) *Equal Opportunties in Colleges and Universities: Towards Better Practices,* Buckingham: SRHE and the Open University Press.

13. *The Guardian* (1995) 20 June.

Chapter 4

Evidence from lead organisations, stakeholders and expert witnesses

4.1   Key findings

- *Under-representation* – there are unacceptably low levels of Black representation at senior levels within the Learning and Skills Council (LSC), the Office for Standards in Education (OFSTED), Her Majesty's Inspectorate (HMI) and the Adult Learning Inspectorate (ALI).

- *Equalities infrastructure* – there are barriers to the progression of Black staff in lead and stakeholder agencies; barriers include isolation, marginalisation, the 'glass ceiling', word-of mouth recruitment, a lack of comprehensive equality procedures and practices.

- *Leadership* – senior managers and individuals in positions of influence need to take personal responsibility for addressing racism and structural barriers.

- *Experience and skills of inspection teams* – unrepresentative inspection teams lack the necessary skills to inspect colleges for race and equalities.

- *Positive action* – targeted positive action schemes should be set up to address the under-representation of Black staff within lead organisations and other key agencies.

- *Trade unions* – good practice examples must be developed to promote awareness of race equality issues in unions.

- *Teacher training* – factors may discourage people from minority ethnic communities from taking up teacher training opportunities.

4.2   Summary of evidence and key themes

A number of key organisations, stakeholders and individual expert witnesses were invited to meet the Commission or to present written evidence during 2000-2001 (see appendix G). The experts were invited because they were identified as having specific knowledge and experience of the sector and race and equalities or because of their organisational expertise in specific organisations. The intention was to enable the Commission to build its evidence base in key areas; to establish the position in the major funding and training bodies regarding the employment of Black staff; and to obtain views about the best way forward for promoting race equality. The meetings provided important opportunities to work in partnership with the sector, to explore ways of tackling racism collectively and to look at some good practice examples. Institutional racism and barriers to the progression of Black staff were issues faced by all the key bodies. Change had to take place internally within lead agencies as they took responsibility for promoting and championing change more broadly. Much common agreement emerged about the issues and strategies needed. The key points from these meetings are outlined below. This evidence also informed the Commission's recommendations to organisations and groups within the sector. These recommendations are set out in chapter 5.

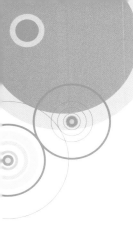

Human resources professionals

Human resources professionals and consultants with expertise in this area highlighted a number of concerns including:

- incorporation resulting in a lower priority for equal opportunities in some colleges

- the lack of rigorous recruitment and selection procedures which meant 'word of mouth' recruitment was still prevalent within the sector

- managers hesitating to set targets for fear of failure

- inspection 'scratching the surface' of equal opportunities issues

- inspection teams rarely matching the college's ethnic profile

- the need for transparent 'equality audits' in colleges to establish the effectiveness of equalities policies and identify the extent of discrimination

- the low status of Black (African-Caribbean) men in the sector compared with other minority ethnic groups.

Further Education National Training Organisation

A survey conducted by the Further Education National Training Organisation amongst its minority ethnic members identified barriers to progression as a key issue for Black staff, characterised or exacerbated by:

- 'the glass ceiling'

- institutional racism

- isolation and marginalisation

- the dismantling of an equality infrastructure following incorporation

- unmet training needs of governors

- lack of information and research into the disproportionate number of Black staff failing probation.

Trade unions

Trade unions provided evidence both of racism within unions and good practice in promoting race equality. Their points echoed many of the comments made in the witness evidence. In addition, they expressed concerns about:

- the difficulties of implementing the union's national policy on racism at a local level

- the need to secure the right leadership to ensure that equalities policies were implemented

- the need for Black staff to feel confident of the union's support when concerns or complaints were raised

- the need for more Black input into unions to redress White, male-dominated structures in some union branches.

Examples of good union practice included:

- the negotiation of joint agreements on guidance for equality and race equality in further education between the Association of Colleges (AOC) and the unions ACM, ATL, GMB, NATFHE, TGWU and UNISON

- the availability of guidance on combating race discrimination and training courses for union representatives to develop skills needed to support individual members facing discrimination

- courses for Black members on how to become more active in the union

- the establishment of a Black members' section and reserved seats for Black members on the union's national executive council

- an ethnic audit of staff and a review of staffing procedures, including equality training in appointment procedures

- a task group established in response to the Stephen Lawrence Inquiry Report

- a union action plan to tackle institutional racism within service groups, with regional offices required to develop action plans monitored by the task group

- a review of case monitoring systems at national and regional level to improve representation of Black members, and possible protocols for the referral of cases from branch to regional level

- training for solicitors on dealing with race discrimination cases

- a major survey of employers to establish what is happening 'on the ground'.

Learning and Skills Development Agency

The Learning and Skills Development Agency (formerly the Further Education Development Agency) described its senior leadership and management training programme as an example of good practice. This was run in partnership with the AOC, with 50% of places reserved for minority ethnic staff, all of whom had completed the programme to date.

Inspectorates

A number of organisations gave evidence about inspections and the role of the different inspectorates, including the Further Education Funding Council (FEFC) inspectorate, OFSTED, and the Trading and Standards Council (TSC). Their evidence coincided with the remodelling of the inspectorates, and the development of the new common inspection framework.

The Further Education Funding Council inspectorate

Key points from the FEFC highlighted that:

- only two full-time Black inspectors were part of the FEFC inspectorate, and that there were no Black senior inspectors

- only 26 out of 354 part-time inspectors were Black[1]

- inspection findings on race and ethnicity were summarised as a report in the *Making a Difference* series (January 2001).

Office for Standards in Education

There were examples of good practice in college responses to cultural and ethnic diversity, with some 99% of colleges in 2000 mentioning race equality in their self-assessment reports. However, the inspectorate agreed that equal opportunities needed to be looked at afresh in the new common inspection framework. The evidence given by OFSTED made reference also to:

- the under-representation of Black staff at senior civil service level[2]

- the increase in Black representation from 2.2% to 3.6% at HMI (inspector) level over the past three years

- the increase in Black representation at administrative level, including significant increases at entry level, from 11% in 1997 to 50% in 2000.

The recruitment of several hundred part-time inspectors provided a further opportunity to increase the number of Black people working for OFSTED. The inspectorate recognised that the inspection plan for colleges should be as clear about staff inclusiveness as it had been about the inclusion of students.[3]

The Training Standards Council

The TSC, which became the ALI in 2000, acknowledged that:

- although the TSC had looked at equal opportunities in colleges, this had been mainly from the perspective of White, male inspectors

- some staff moving from the FEFC and TSC to the new LSC may not have the right skills to respond to the new equality agenda

- secondments of Black staff to the inspectorate would help increase representation.

The TSC's vision of high quality provision was regarded positively because it was driven by the needs of individual learners, not by the needs of providers, and was more 'equal opportunities friendly'.

Further Education Funding Council

The FEFC talked about three reports which had provided a framework within which colleges could develop their equalities policies and practices. The national inquiry reports were: *Inclusive Learning*, the report of the Tomlinson committee (1996); *Learning Works - Widening Participation in Further Education*, the report of the Kennedy committee (1997); and *Further Education and Equality* (1998). The Council made particular reference to the position of part-time staff in colleges, drawing the Commission's attention to:

- increased use of part-time staff to improve flexibility and efficiency

- often cursory recruitment procedures for hourly paid staff

- lack of consistent support for some groups of staff, especially hourly paid and support staff, and the important role of the team leader.[4]

The Learning and Skills Council

The LSC assumed statutory responsibility for all post-16 education and training in April 2001. Promoting equality of opportunity is central to the Council's vision 'to create a learning society free from discrimination and prejudice … which encourages all learners to reach their full potential'. The Council is charged by the Secretary of State to mainstream equality of opportunity into all its policies, programmes and actions.

The LSC is a significant national employer, with some 5000 staff in its Coventry office and 47 local offices. The Council acknowledged that staffing in some local offices did not always reflect adequately the local ethnic profile. Work is in hand, in partnership with the Commission for Racial Equality (CRE) to identify a process to increase representation. Strategies include regional 'road-shows' and advertising in the minority ethnic press.

Department for Education and Employment
(now the Department for Education and Skills)

The division at the DfEE responsible for equal opportunities in relation to the LSC also gave evidence to the Commission. The point was made that in making public appointments of LSC and local LSC members, equal opportunities was included as one of the criteria against which candidates were assessed. However, an evaluation of the appointments process was underway. The Commission was provided with a breakdown of the figures of LSC appointments of people from a minority ethnic background, as set out below.

LSC appointments: breakdown of people from a minority ethnic background

(Data submitted February 2001)

Position appointed	No. of positions	No. of minority ethnic applications	No. of minority ethnic appointments
National chair	1	3	0
National chief executive	1	3	0
National council and youth and adult committee members	33	272	3
Local chairs	47	27	3
Local executive directors	47	37	1
Local council members	587	227	41
TOTAL	716	569	48

The figures show an unacceptable level of Black representation in all positions.

The Teacher Training Agency

The Teacher Training Agency (TTA) promotes teaching as a profession and aims to ensure adequate numbers of suitably qualified people enrol and complete teacher training each year. The TTA presented its findings from recent research into the factors that influenced people from minority ethnic

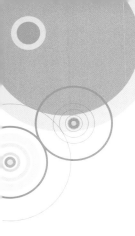

communities coming forward to train as teachers. Many of the factors were of particular interest to the Commission, including:

- the proximity of training opportunities to centres of minority ethnic population, which was seen as a critical factor in attracting Black trainees

- the need to balance efforts to increase the number of Black trainees against the use of impartial selection criteria; this was a sensitive issue – trainees stated categorically that they would resent any overt relaxation of entry conditions which might label them as being of a lower professional standard than their White colleagues

- one in six survey respondents had experiences of racial harassment in their first teaching posts, particularly from pupils.

Some trainees were motivated by their belief that minority ethnic pupils would benefit from the presence of more Black teachers in schools. However, others had pointed out that the pressure to act as a role model added to the stress of school placements. Trainees felt it was important not to assume that coming from a similar background to a pupil was sufficient to win their respect. Like their White colleagues, newly-qualified Black teachers felt they had not received appropriate training to work with certain groups of pupils, such as African-Caribbean boys at risk of exclusion.

Policy Studies Institute

The Commission was keen to compare the situation in further education with that in higher education. The Policy Studies Institute presented its findings from a survey of ethnicity and employment in higher education.[5] The key points below are taken from a fuller summary in appendix F:

- 6.5% of academic staff in UK higher education institutions were from non-White backgrounds

- Black staff were less likely to be professors and more likely to be on fixed-term contracts, part-time, and less senior posts, particularly women

- only 5% of the sample had a positive action plan for minority ethnic groups

- one in five respondents had experienced discrimination in job applications.

The Commission concluded that both further and higher education had few senior Black staff, with Black staff over-represented in part-time, relatively junior posts.

Other government agencies

A number of agencies external to the sector were keen to share good practice ideas with the Commission and discuss how they approached the implementation of an equalities agenda within their own organisations.

Inland Revenue

Evidence from the Inland Revenue stressed the absolute necessity of clear and firm leadership on equalities, as a pre-condition for achieving change. The department's diversity plans had been rated as excellent by the Cabinet. The first conference for minority ethnic staff had been convened recently by the department. Key themes in the successful pursuit of any diversity strategy were highlighted:

- the need for all staff, particularly managers, to be accountable for promoting diversity
- the need for all departments to have diversity plans in place
- the need for specific time-limited targets for under-represented groups
- the possibility of using incentives for performance on meeting equality objectives
- the need for active use of positive action initiatives such as targeted mentoring schemes and secondment schemes
- the need to make steady progress on equality rather than attempting 'quick fix' solutions.

Home Office

The Home Office's evidence to the Commission focused on initiatives to tackle the under-representation of Black staff in senior civil service positions.

Minority ethnic network

In 1997, the Home Office identified through staff surveys and focus groups that people from minority ethnic groups were experiencing discrimination throughout all government departments and agencies. They found that their chances of promotion were fewer than their White counterparts and that only a few had had the opportunity to work in the policy department, though not in high profile roles. Figures published in 1998 showed that minority ethnic groups were under-represented in senior grades. Following a senior management conference in 1998, a race equality action plan was put in place, which included the offer of support and funding for a network for minority ethnic staff. The *Stephen Lawrence Inquiry Report* and the Home Secretary's commitment to target the recruitment, promotion and retention of minority ethnic staff were two important initiatives in driving change.

Other initiatives

Other initiatives taken by the Home Office, the Immigration and Nationality Directorate and the Immigration Service included:

- the establishment of an ethnic minority monitoring group, with representatives from the CRE, to provide an independent check on action being taken
- a CRE employers' standards audit of all Home Office systems and procedures
- a review of the department's equal opportunities complaints' scheme, involving consultation on new schemes, such as a pilot harassment contact officer scheme.

Notes

1. Figures correct as at January 2001.
2. This covers Her Majesty's Chief Inspector (HMCI) Directorate of Inspections and the senior management team.
3. OFSTED, October 2000.
4. *FEFC National Report from the Inspectorate 1999 – 2000: Supporting Part-Time Teachers in Further Education.*
5. Carter J, Fenton, S and Modood T (1999) *Ethnicity and employment in higher education,* London: Policy Studies Institute.

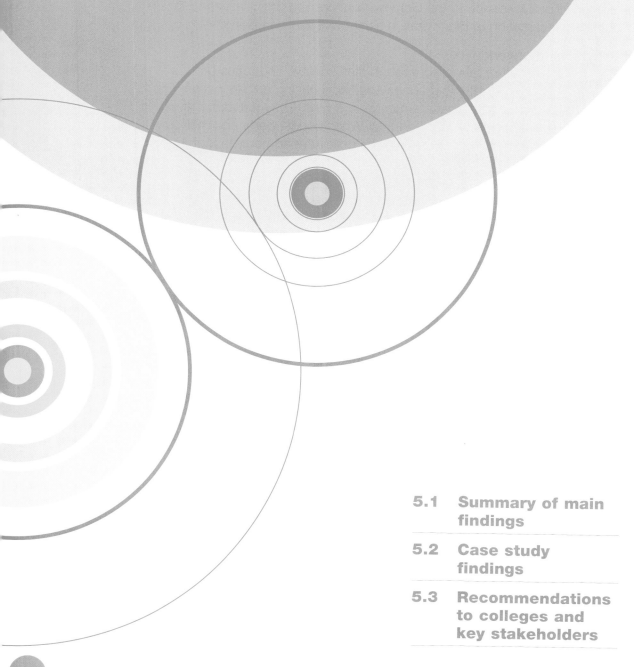

Chapter

5

Findings and recommendations

The full report of the Commission for Black Staff in Further Education

5.1　Summary of main findings

In the last chapter of the report, the Commission lists its main findings and makes recommendations for action. The Commission wishes to see urgent action by national organisations, colleges and individuals to tackle the issues that prevent Black staff from playing their full, valuable part in further education. It also wants to see forward-looking inclusive colleges recognised for their efforts to break down the barriers to racial equality for staff and students. A speaking tour aimed at colleges is also being organised. National and local LSC events and other key conferences will provide the Commission with the opportunity to disseminate findings. The Commission wishes to see the momentum for change at all levels within the sector, within individual colleges and in a range of organisations, harnessed, driven forward and sustained.

The Commission published a summary report of its findings in July 2002.

The key findings of the Commission's work are outlined below.

Staff numbers

- Black staff constituted 6.9% of the overall staff population in further education colleges.

- Black staff were under-represented in certain regions. In London 25.5% of staff were Black compared with a minority ethnic population of 28%; in the North West, 1.2% of staff were Black compared with a minority ethnic population of 4%; and in the West Midlands, 8.3% of staff were Black compared with a minority ethnic population of 10%.

Employment status

- There were only four Black principals constituting fewer than 1% of the cohort.

- At managerial level Black staff constituted 4.9% of managers, 3.8% of heads of teaching departments and 4.6% of senior lecturers. In comparison, 6.9% of all main grade lecturers were Black.

- Only 6% of all Black staff were managers compared with 9% of White staff.

- Seven per cent of staff in teaching positions were Black.

- Black lecturing staff were over-represented in part-time lecturing posts (8.5%) and under-represented in the more secure fractional posts (4.5%).

- 7.2% of support staff directly employed by further education colleges were Black. (This did not include staff working in catering, cleaning, security and other services when these were contracted out to other organisations.)

- Twenty-five per cent of staff working in contracted organisations were Black.

- In contracted positions, Black staff were three times more likely than White staff to be employed in security posts.

- Sixty-five per cent of White staff were in permanent teaching positions, compared with only 60% of Black staff.

Staff qualifications

- Fifty-five per cent of minority ethnic staff in further education were educated to first degree level compared with 49% of White staff.

- Six per cent of minority ethnic staff had no formal qualifications, whereas 8% of White further education staff were similarly unqualified.

Curriculum

- Black lecturers were concentrated disproportionately in particular curriculum areas and were more likely to be employed in continuing education (including literacy and numeracy and English for Speakers of Other Languages), and, to a lesser extent, in maths and science departments.

Sector employment policies and procedures

The national survey (2001) showed:

- Fewer than half (42%) of further education colleges always used formal recruitment procedures when appointing part-time hourly paid teaching staff.

- Fewer than one in five of colleges nationally used target setting to address the under-representation of Black staff.

- Fifteen per cent of colleges set targets for the employment and progression of Black staff.

- Twenty per cent of colleges set targets for representation in governing bodies.

- Five per cent of colleges set objectives for representation on key college committees, such as academic boards.

- Fewer than one in five colleges monitored the employment policies of contractors.

- Eleven per cent of colleges included Black representatives on interview panels as standard practice.

- Fifty-three per cent of colleges used ethnic monitoring data.

- Fewer than half of all colleges (45%) had specific equality training programmes for staff.

- The majority of colleges did not have Black staff support or development groups; only 8% of institutions had these groups and only 1% of colleges had a mentoring programme specifically for Black staff.

Equality policies

- Six per cent of colleges nationally did not have an equal opportunities policy.

- Only 6% of colleges had a specific race equality policy before the Race Relations Amendment Act was implemented.

- Just over half of colleges (52%) had specific equality procedures that addressed the recruitment, selection, induction and progression of staff.

- Eighteen per cent of colleges had specific equality policies or criteria relating to redundancies and/or restructuring.

Governors

- A survey of 270 members of the Clerks' Network provided responses from 134 colleges. It revealed that 8% of governors and only one corporation clerk were Black. Fifty-eight colleges (43%) had no Black governors at all.

Students numbers

- The percentage of minority ethnic students in further education in England had increased from 12% in 1997-1998 to 14% in 1999-2000.

- There was substantial regional variation in the number of minority ethnic students. For example:

London	39%
West Midlands	15.6%
North East	4.3%
South West	4.2%

- Four fifths of young people from minority ethnic groups remained in the education system compared to just over two thirds of White young people.

- Twenty-two per cent of White further education students lived in deprived areas, defined in relation to levels of unemployment, crime, public housing and local access to health, education and a better physical environment. The proportion of students from minority ethnic groups living in deprived areas was far higher:

Bangladeshi	76%
Black African	73%
Pakistani	68%
Black Caribbean	67%
Black 'other'	64%

Student achievement

- Minority ethnic students were still underachieving in comparison with their White counterparts, with all minority ethnic groups attaining lower grades, despite a marked improvement in achievement for all minority ethnic groups.

Inspection

- The Further Education Funding Council (2001) revealed that there were only two full-time Black inspectors (3%), and no senior Black inspectors.

- Twenty-six out of a total of 354 part-time inspectors were Black representing 7%.

- Evidence from the Office for Standards in Education (OFSTED) (2001) revealed that the profile of minority ethnic staff had changed considerably since 1997 at certain levels.

- At senior civil service level there had been no change, with no Black staff employed.

- At HMI (inspector) level, minority ethnic staff had increased from 2.2% in 1997 to 3.6% in 2000.

- In Band A, which covered senior administration posts in OFSTED, minority ethnic staff made up 11% of total staff in 1997; this had increased to 18.2% in June 2000.

- In Band B, the next administration grade down, there were no staff from minority ethnic groups in 1997; by June 2000 that figure had risen to 11.1%.

- The most significant change had taken place at the lowest administrative grade (entry level), where minority ethnic staff constituted 11% of staff in 1997; in 2000, 50% of staff coming in at entrance level were from minority ethnic groups.

5.2   Case study findings

These findings relate to the eight case study colleges included in the national survey.

Recruitment and selection

- Black staff tended to be more critical than White staff of the effectiveness of their institution's equality policies. Twice as many Black (27%) as White staff thought that their college's equality recruitment policies were 'ineffective'.

- Forty-five per cent of Black staff, compared with 58% White staff, stated that such policies were 'moderately effective'.

Conditions of service

- Black staff had less access than White staff to working conditions conducive to equality. These included flexible working hours, job sharing, parental leave, working from home, workplace nurseries, and facilities for prayer at work.

- There were differences between Black and White staff in the practices followed when they wanted a day off to fulfil caring responsibilities or to attend a religious or cultural festival. Black staff were more likely to use paid or unpaid leave, while White staff were more likely to take time off which they would make up later.

Job satisfaction

- Overall, the majority of staff, both Black and White, expressed a degree of satisfaction with their work.

- Black staff expressed lower levels of satisfaction on almost all measures compared with White staff (ranging from the sense of achievement derived from work to the feeling that they were respected by managers).

Career development

- All staff, especially Black staff, felt that relationships with their line managers were very important in affecting career progression: positive relationships were instrumental to good progression; negative relationships could block progression.

- Black staff were more likely than White staff to report feeling blocked in their progression.

- Black staff were less satisfied with equality policies relating to staff development and training and were less likely than White staff to consider them effective.

Equality policies and practices

- An active and genuine commitment from senior managers was seen as important if progress was to be made on equality issues. However, fewer than 20% of Black respondents, and fewer than 40% of White respondents, felt that their college had a senior management team that actively promoted race equality; provided training in race equality or dealing with racist incidents; or actively supported staff who complained of racism or other forms of discrimination. Few staff felt that their college consulted staff in the development of equality policies.

- Black and White staff perceived their college ethos in strikingly different ways. Only 37% of Black staff compared with 62% of White staff stated that their college welcomed and valued all groups of staff.

- Fewer than half of Black staff (43%) but almost four fifths of White staff (78%) felt that their college offered real equality of opportunity for employees irrespective of race, gender, disability, religious or cultural background.

- Almost one third (30%) of Black staff reported experiencing direct disadvantage or discrimination because of their 'race'.

Retention and future employment

- Over half of all respondents expected to change jobs within five years, although Black Caribbean women were the least likely to be able to foresee such a change.

- Of the Black African Caribbean men who thought they would change their job within the following five years, 95% indicated they would also change their employer.

- More Black staff (43%) than White staff (38.8%) had jobs that they considered 'too stressful'.

- Black staff in particular highlighted a lack of promotion opportunities and experiences of racism and discrimination as factors that would encourage them to leave their jobs.

- Black staff were more likely to identify poor conditions of employment including lack of job security, inflexible working hours, lack of resources to do their jobs and attitudes of colleagues as factors influencing their decision to leave their job. Poor or 'bullying' management styles emerged as an important factor in focus groups.

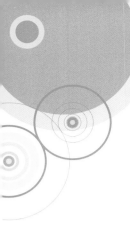

5.3 Recommendations to colleges and key stakeholders

The Commission proposes that immediate action be taken by stakeholder organisations, sector agencies, college corporations, managers and individual staff on the following key recommendations.

Department for Education and Skills

The Department for Education and Skills (DfES) should:

- provide clear and decisive leadership by modelling best race equality practice as an employer

- monitor the impact of the Learning and Skills Act 2001 (section 14), and use its responsibility to interpret the Secretary of State's remit letter to the Learning and Skills Council (LSC), ensuring its race equality objectives are translated into ambitious and realistic targets, and then implemented

- require the director of the proposed Leadership College to embed best race equality practice in all its activities and ensure that its programmes equip participants to manage diversity in the learning and skills sector

- work with the LSC to enable all college corporations to set race equality employment targets measured against appropriate benchmarks by July 2003, for incremental implementation by 2009

- ensure that adequate funding is available to:

    - equip all college staff to manage effectively and deliver race equality

    - provide fast-track management training for suitably qualified minority ethnic staff

    - make full appropriate use of positive action in staff training and recruitment

    - market careers in post-compulsory training and education as a desirable career option to minority ethnic communities

    - fund other measures such as mentoring and ethnic minority achievement grants that contribute to raising the achievement of minority ethnic learners.

- ensure that the boards of all DfES-funded bodies are representative of the diversity of the national population; and that the LSC, in particular, becomes fully representative of the profile of learners in the sector

- ensure that the new Standards Unit in the Adult Skills Directorate mainstreams equalities in all its guidance, programmes, learning materials and actions

- devise and fund a robust three-year strategy to implement the recommendations of the Commission for Black Staff in Further Education and report its progress to the Secretary of State

- ensure that its race equality scheme is exemplary and implemented systematically.

The Learning and Skills Council

The LSC should:

- provide clear and decisive leadership by modelling best race equality practice as an employer

- address the under-representation of Black people on its staff and take systematic steps to ensure that its workforce at all levels is fully representative of the ethnic profile of the national population by 2009

- ensure that its national and local councils, its chief executive, national directors, local executive directors and other senior staff receive high quality race equality training as required by the Race Relations (Amendment) Act 2000

- take systematic action to ensure that all college corporation members receive race equality training and encourage the sharing of good practice by governing bodies across the sector

- take action for targeted recruitment and training of minority ethnic governors

- ensure that its external equality and diversity advisory group is fully representative of race equality interests

- work in partnership with the Commission for Racial Equality (CRE) to issue definitive guidance to learning providers on how to translate the requirements of the Race Relations (Amendment) Act 2000 into meaningful learner and staff recruitment targets

- ensure that the implementation of race equality targets and training is adequately funded

- expand the *Staff Individualised Record* to include all employment grades and pay levels, including hourly paid staff, so that the position and progress of minority ethnic staff can be accurately measured

- require the external advisory group making recommendations on the final content of the revised framework for the provider performance review to advise on how best the review process can support colleges to meet their statutory duties under the Race Relations Amendment Act 2000

- set up a 'beacon award' scheme to recognise excellence in race equality practice

- require its management board to ensure that its race equality scheme is exemplary and implemented systematically.

Inspectorates

Inspectorates should:

- provide clear and decisive leadership, by modelling employment best practice in their own staff

- address, as a matter of urgency, the under-representation of Black people in their staff at all levels so that they are able to provide inspection teams reflective of the national population and of the local communities of the learning providers they inspect, by setting race equality employment targets measured against appropriate benchmarks by July 2003 for incremental implementation by 2009

- add a separate, additional equalities question to the seven common inspection framework questions and report on it
- ensure that inspection reports evaluate the implementation of race and equalities policies and highlight good practice
- report on the representation of minority ethnic groups in learner and staff recruitment and progression
- ensure that all inspectors understand their critical leadership role in promoting race equality
- ensure that board members, as well as the chief executive, senior staff and the executive receive race equality training
- deliver mandatory annual equalities training for all inspectors so they are fully equipped to identify and report on progress towards race equality within the revised common inspection framework
- ensure that their boards are representative of the profile of learners in the sector
- ensure that their race equality schemes are exemplary and implemented systematically.

Colleges

College corporations should:

- provide clear and decisive leadership, by modelling best race equality practice as employers
- incorporate into their annual training cycle an explicit component on their statutory and other responsibilities for race equality
- ensure that the composition of the corporation board reflects the ethnic diversity of communities both locally and nationally
- ensure that external and internal recruitment processes actively promote applications from Black staff and governors
- ensure that the principal and senior staff set race equality employment targets measured against appropriate benchmarks by July 2003, for incremental implementation by 2009
- ensure that senior postholder performance appraisal schemes incorporate race equality targets
- ensure that senior managers incorporate race equality specifications into contracts with service providers
- ensure that all governors who sit on appointment panels for senior staff have received appropriate race equality training
- ensure that formal recruitment procedures are adopted for all posts (including part-time staff) unless there are exceptional circumstances; assess the reasons for the success or failure of minority ethnic candidates, and act on those findings
- require training for all clerks to enable them to advise corporations on their legal obligations under the Race Relations (Amendment) Act 2000
- ensure that their race equality policies are exemplary and implemented systematically.

College leadership

Principals and chief executives should:

- lead and inspire the college on implementing equalities objectives and actively promote the college's race equality policy internally and externally

- seek to refine their personal and professional understanding of equalities issues through training and continuous professional development

- oversee and report on a rigorous action plan to achieve the college's objectives, as identified in its race equality policy

- ensure that equalities objectives and considerations are embedded in the policies and practices of the institution, and that all staff are aware of their individual and collective roles in ensuring an inclusive learning environment

- ensure that the senior management team is accountable, and that all managers understand their responsibility to implement the race equality policy consistently across the college

- ensure that staff development is available to ensure compliance with the legislation and promote appropriate action in cases of race discrimination

- ensure that performance appraisal schemes for all staff incorporate a race equality component

- ensure that Black staff are supported through the establishment of focus groups, the development of mentoring schemes and/or affiliation to appropriate national networks

- set equalities targets that are ambitious and proportionate to local communities' needs, in consultation with learners and staff from those communities

- make arrangements for systematic ethnic monitoring of learners and staff, and for regular reports to the corporation ensuring that results are published annually for public scrutiny

- ensure that staff recruitment processes are open and transparent and operate within rigorous equalities guidelines.

Management

College managers should:

- actively promote race equality and good race relations

- be responsible and accountable for implementing the college's race equality policy and procedures

- ensure that all full and part-time staff know their individual responsibilities and particular role in implementing the race equality policy, and receive appropriate support and training in carrying them out

- provide leadership at sectional and departmental level to champion equalities in general, and race equality in particular

- ensure that appraisal schemes incorporate race equality targets or criteria

- ensure that all staff recruitment is carried out in accordance with the college's race equality policy

- actively share good race equality practice in the teaching, learning and support of learners

- take appropriate action where staff and learners contravene the college's race equality policy

- keep up-to-date with race relations and other relevant legislation, and maximise training and learning opportunities for their staff.

Staff

Full and part-time college staff should:

- actively promote race equality and good race relations

- take account of their individual responsibilities and particular roles in implementing the race equality policy, and receive appropriate support and training in carrying them out

- avoid discrimination against colleagues or learners for reasons of race, colour, nationality or ethnic or national origin

- be able to recognise and tackle racial bias and stereotyping

- keep up-to-date with race relations and other relevant legislation, and participate in relevant training and learning opportunities

- monitor, record and respond effectively to racist incidents

- promote the advantages of ethnic and cultural diversity both locally and nationally through their teaching and support roles.

Trade unions

Trade unions should:

- provide clear and decisive leadership, by modelling best race equality practice as employers

- set race equality employment targets for trade union staff, representatives and lay officers measured against appropriate benchmarks by July 2003, for incremental implementation by 2009

- ensure that, at every level, their union's publicly stated commitment to race equality is fully reflected in the actions of paid officials and lay officers

- include specific reference to race equality in their strategic and action planning cycles

- incorporate race equality into the formal negotiating arrangements they have with employers

- ensure that paid officials and lay officers recognise the needs of their Black members and actively support them in casework arising from acts of institutional and individual racism

- ensure that paid officials and lay officers involved in casework receive race equality training

- share good race equality practice nationally, locally and between unions and union members.

Other agencies

National and local sector agencies, skills sector councils and other stakeholders should:

- provide clear and decisive leadership, by modelling best race equality practice as employers

- take steps to ensure that their staffing reflects the national population and the learners served by the learning and skills sector by setting race equality employment targets for their staff, measured against appropriate benchmarks by July 2003, for incremental implementation by 2009

- recognise, promote and reward best race equality practice

- ensure that all staff receive appropriate race and equalities training and are aware of the different needs of the Black communities served by the learning and skills sector

- ensure that staff are trained and able to comply with race relations legislation governing employers who provide work-based learning.

The Commission for Racial Equality

The CRE should:

- work with the LSC and DfES on improving ethnic monitoring systems and on developing and implementing targets for learners and staff

- actively support all agencies in the learning and skills sector in implementing their race equality schemes

- publish an enforcement strategy in support of the Race Relations (Amendment) Act 2000 that clarifies when and how the sector could become the subject of enforcement action.

Partnership working

All agencies working in the learning and skills sector should endeavour to work collaboratively to ensure that race equality best practice is adopted and widely shared.

Continuing the work of the Commission

The Comission for Black Staff in Further Education hopes to see its work continue after January 2003 through:

- a stakeholders' group set up jointly by the LSC and DfES, incorporating all of the key bodies in the further education sector – this body will take responsibility for developing a strategy to implement the recommendations of the Commission

- the establishment of an equalities commission for the sector to promote and monitor the progress made by colleges and stakeholder organisations.

Note

The Commission's summary report: *An agenda for action* is available from www.feonline.net.

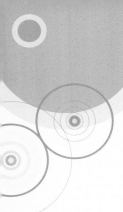

Appendix A:
Witness events

In order to begin the process of collecting evidence in the sector the Commission decided to hold a number of key witness events around the country between October 2000 and June 2001.

The Commission also supported a Race Equality and Diversity Focus Group Event on 28th June 2001 at Hackney Community College. This one-day event was initiated by the college and organised in conjunction with Equality Works (an equal opportunities training organisation) and the Commission.

Nine college witness days were held:

12th October 2000	Matthew Boulton College, Birmingham
15th November	Greenwich Community College (formerly Woolwich College), London
13th December	Bournemouth and Poole College, Bournemouth
31st January 2001	Oldham College, Oldham
15th February	Notre Dame Sixth Form College, Leeds
8th March	Newcastle College, Newcastle
5th April	Leicester College, Leicester
10th May	Bradford College, Bradford
11th June	Westminster/Kingsway College, London
28th June	Hackney Focus Event, Hackney Community College, London

Appendix B:
Commission for Racial Equality website

The Commission for Racial Equality (CRE) website **www.cre.gov.uk** includes *The duty to promote race equality: A Guide for Further and Higher Education Institutions (Non-statutory)*. The guidance supports the CRE's statutory Code of Practice on the Duty to Promote Race Equality. It is mainly for the governing bodies of further education and higher education institutions that are bound by the legislative duties. Unlike the Code, the guide does not have legal standing. Nevertheless, the CRE explains that the guide is important as it is 'based on tried and tested experience in FE and HE institutions that have been working towards race equality.' The guide includes:

- an explanation of the benefits of complying with the general duty to promote race equality

- an explanation of the scope of the general and specific duties, including what the general duty means in practice

- an explanation of the specific duties, including useful examples of colleges' experiences

- an outline of the specific duties that arise in the employment field, which, although not applicable to further education colleges, are applicable to some institutions in the further education sector (e.g. Learning and Skills Council and the Higher Education Funding Council for England)

- an appendix which explains a framework for a race equality policy

- a guide to the Race Relations Act 1976.

Appendix C:
Ethnic breakdown of the population across unitary and local authority districts

Unitary authority/local authority district by ethnic origin: Winter 2000-2001										
Figures for areas in England[1]										Not seasonally adjusted
	District	Total[2]	White	Mixed	Asian or Asian British	Black or Black British	Chinese	Other ethnic group	Total Minority Ethnic inc "Other"[3]	Total of Known Ethnicity[4]	Minorit Ethnic %age Known Ethnici
1	Newham	242,910	81,469	11,046	104,290	35,156	460	10,489	161,441	242,910	66.46%
2	Brent	249,717	100,166	2,285	78,117	54,247	2,614	12,288	149,551	249,717	59.89%
3	Tower Hamlets	183,562	79,634	1,522	84,178	13,046	1,748	3,434	103,928	183,562	56.62%
4	Ealing	311,754	174,134	3,620	85,130	36,063	3,056	9,751	137,620	311,754	44.14%
5	Harrow	211,282	121,043	863	71,643	13,255	0	4,478	90,239	211,282	42.71%
6	Hackney	198,583	113,784	6,202	24,123	47,336	3,744	2,920	84,325	198,109	42.56%
7	Redbridge	229,990	143,583	3,344	57,791	19,352	3,786	2,134	86,407	229,990	37.57%
8	Leicester	277,964	174,991	5,369	83,249	10,708	3,210	437	102,973	277,964	37.05%
9	Southwark	242,878	155,860	7,592	11,352	62,847	2,469	2,403	86,663	242,523	35.73%
10	Lewisham	240,429	156,503	10,144	12,836	48,771	8,237	3,938	83,926	240,429	34.91%
11	Croydon	333,685	222,302	10,302	35,314	54,728	1,345	9,362	111,051	333,353	33.31%
12	Lambeth	278,055	185,344	4,772	5,978	72,772	1,013	7,736	92,271	277,615	33.24%
13	Westminster	264,559	179,926	9,133	14,140	25,528	10,087	25,745	84,633	264,559	31.99%
14	Slough	106,293	72,459	3,136	24,388	5,239	0	1,071	33,834	106,293	31.83%
15	Birmingham	999,867	681,942	29,141	198,440	73,647	11,457	4,364	317,049	998,991	31.74%
16	Camden	213,303	147,243	11,362	25,399	15,331	4,172	9,796	66,060	213,303	30.97%
17	Hounslow	210,406	146,947	4,685	43,114	8,140	3,623	3,897	63,459	210,406	30.16%
18	Waltham Forest	211,709	150,353	9,342	18,211	30,349	474	2,980	61,356	211,709	28.98%
19	Kensington and Chelsea	210,778	153,668	8,938	10,253	18,646	0	18,250	56,087	209,755	26.74%
20	Wolverhampton	235,530	173,235	3,516	45,313	11,251	0	2,215	62,295	235,530	26.45%
21	Haringey	220,883	161,951	2,019	10,688	31,074	2,380	11,983	58,144	220,095	26.42%
22	Merton	192,033	141,341	4,573	20,535	20,495	480	4,609	50,692	192,033	26.40%

	District	Total[2]	White	Mixed	Asian or Asian British	Black or Black British	Chinese	Other ethnic group	Total Minority Ethnic inc "Other"[3]	Total of Known Ethnicity[4]	Minority Ethnic as %age of Known Ethnicity
23	Wandsworth	270,423	205,328	6,729	22,272	27,447	598	8,049	65,095	270,423	24.07%
24	Hillingdon	254,458	194,608	6,621	40,724	10,937	0	1,096	59,378	253,986	23.38%
25	Hammersmith and Fulham	164,983	127,275	2,480	12,702	12,360	883	9,283	37,708	164,983	22.86%
26	Islington	169,759	131,854	3,217	1,508	27,870	1,225	4,085	37,905	169,759	22.33%
27	Barnet	347,576	271,217	10,015	37,965	15,958	3,268	9,153	76,359	347,576	21.97%
28	Manchester	450,483	354,611	16,082	30,951	32,528	5,706	10,605	95,872	450,483	21.28%
29	Enfield	269,321	212,068	4,653	18,087	29,375	481	4,657	57,253	269,321	21.26%
30	Bradford	483,279	381,858	6,762	86,632	7,232	0	795	101,421	483,279	20.99%
31	Barking and Dagenham	154,259	123,847	5,729	9,842	14,411	0	430	30,412	154,259	19.71%
32	Greenwich	219,263	178,245	2,335	10,168	26,490	1,084	498	40,575	218,820	18.54%
33	Luton	179,616	147,100	3,456	20,154	8,540	0	366	32,516	179,616	18.10%
34	Sandwell	282,815	233,046	1,291	42,359	6,119	0	0	49,769	282,815	17.60%
35	Watford	79,598	65,734	1,110	3,675	4,902	1,150	3,027	13,864	79,598	17.42%
36	Kingston upon Thames	152,962	126,027	3,127	17,607	5,325	414	0	26,473	152,500	17.36%
37	Pendle	80,901	67,365	477	13,059	0	0	0	13,536	80,901	16.73%
38	Nottingham	272,626	227,302	5,422	20,485	15,756	3,661	0	45,324	272,626	16.62%
39	City of London	9,649	8,107	0	0	0	645	897	1,542	9,649	15.98%
40	Walsall	257,490	218,437	2,784	31,845	2,897	0	1,527	39,053	257,490	15.17%
41	Kirklees	395,130	336,019	5,711	46,932	4,694	457	1,317	59,111	395,130	14.96%
42	Oldham	213,182	182,703	499	26,733	1,966	421	860	30,479	213,182	14.30%
43	Bedford	146,686	126,380	3,762	14,144	1,959	0	441	20,306	146,686	13.84%
44	Blackburn with Darwen	132,673	114,980	416	17,277	0	0	0	17,693	132,673	13.34%
45	Cambridge	123,992	108,331	2,013	10,702	0	0	2,946	15,661	123,992	12.63%
46	Oxford	151,783	132,752	2,337	6,854	7,208	2,632	0	19,031	151,783	12.54%
47	Reading	143,002	124,606	10,115	2,886	3,786	0	824	17,611	142,217	12.38%
48	Crawley	95,281	83,572	2,103	8,273	866	0	467	11,709	95,281	12.29%
49	Sutton	177,867	157,614	3,614	9,110	5,322	794	931	19,771	177,385	11.15%
50	Coventry	293,345	260,974	6,904	16,588	3,093	1,484	4,302	32,371	293,345	11.04%
51	Hertsmere	98,961	88,313	817	7,255	1,630	0	946	10,648	98,961	10.76%
52	Bromley	305,578	273,027	5,254	10,514	10,548	4,232	2,003	32,551	305,578	10.65%

	District	Total[2]	White	Mixed	Asian or Asian British	Black or Black British	Chinese	Other ethnic group	Total Minority Ethnic inc "Other"[3]	Total of Known Ethnicity[4]	Minority Ethnic %age of Known Ethnicity
53	Rochdale	210,860	189,530	1,334	18,982	507	0	507	21,330	210,860	10.12%
54	Ipswich	111,029	99,805	1,051	6,382	1,980	0	1,811	11,224	111,029	10.11%
55	Stevenage	80,322	72,373	720	5,709	0	1,520	0	7,949	80,322	9.90%
56	Milton Keynes	212,424	192,431	1,506	2,923	11,648	3,104	812	19,993	212,424	9.41%
57	Preston	133,043	120,819	495	9,965	0	1,764	0	12,224	133,043	9.19%
58	Wycombe	159,920	145,347	4,625	7,267	1,937	0	744	14,573	159,920	9.11%
59	Derby	234,012	213,593	2,355	13,645	4,008	411	0	20,419	234,012	8.73%
60	Leeds	717,422	656,128	11,760	33,159	10,852	3,470	1,719	60,960	717,088	8.50%
61	Richmond upon Thames	198,697	181,507	3,033	5,058	4,252	474	3,781	16,598	198,105	8.38%
62	Northampton	191,644	175,731	1,738	8,765	4,464	427	519	15,913	191,644	8.30%
63	Wokingham	140,719	129,577	2,066	6,520	1,698	858	0	11,142	140,719	7.92%
64	Purbeck	45,487	41,957	2,680	0	455	0	395	3,530	45,487	7.76%
65	Bristol, City of	407,262	375,339	8,025	4,713	15,909	0	2,721	31,368	406,707	7.71%
66	Aylesbury Vale	160,869	148,481	1,472	10,099	817	0	0	12,388	160,869	7.70%
67	Gloucester	110,217	101,759	2,306	3,522	2,165	0	465	8,458	110,217	7.67%
68	Calderdale	191,190	176,568	3,135	9,035	2,075	377	0	14,622	191,190	7.65%
69	Bolton	264,335	244,148	470	17,804	1,913	0	0	20,187	264,335	7.64%
70	Sheffield	524,551	484,743	6,464	26,531	4,777	0	2,036	39,808	524,551	7.59%
71	Trafford	215,779	200,868	1,255	8,977	4,679	0	0	14,911	215,779	6.91%
72	Warwick	125,828	117,164	1,420	6,348	514	382	0	8,664	125,828	6.89%
73	Southampton	208,945	194,181	3,332	5,813	2,497	2,322	0	13,964	208,145	6.71%
74	Epsom and Ewell	71,192	66,428	441	3,913	0	0	410	4,764	71,192	6.69%
75	Hyndburn	76,143	70,691	0	4,629	0	0	437	5,066	75,757	6.69%
76	Brentwood	69,998	65,358	2,173	2,467	0	0	0	4,640	69,998	6.63%
77	Three Rivers	94,930	88,644	1,092	3,260	1,242	0	692	6,286	94,930	6.62%
78	Chiltern	90,440	84,525	402	3,923	0	408	1,182	5,915	90,440	6.54%
79	Telford and Wrekin	149,240	139,525	2,597	4,762	846	1,510	0	9,715	149,240	6.51%
80	Blaby	89,169	83,573	323	3,842	311	758	362	5,596	89,169	6.28%
81	Elmbridge	137,418	128,942	0	5,568	0	0	2,908	8,476	137,418	6.17%
82	Havering	233,935	219,626	2,734	5,373	3,343	2,366	493	14,309	233,935	6.12%
83	Burnley	84,315	79,246	0	4,253	389	0	427	5,069	84,315	6.01%

Appendix C: Ethnic breakdown of the population across unitary and local authority districts

	District	Total[2]	White	Mixed	Asian or Asian British	Black or Black British	Chinese	Other ethnic group	Total Minority Ethnic inc "Other"[3]	Total of Known Ethnicity[4]	Minority Ethnic as %age of Known Ethnicity
84	Basingstoke and Deane	149,682	140,251	1,672	3,564	1,708	988	990	8,922	149,173	5.98%
85	Charnwood	158,379	149,087	383	7,626	402	0	881	9,292	158,379	5.87%
86	Rossendale	61,840	58,246	789	2,040	0	765	0	3,594	61,840	5.81%
87	Bury	179,703	169,374	1,141	9,188	0	0	0	10,329	179,703	5.75%
88	Windsor and Maidenhead	141,412	133,356	0	4,828	0	0	3,228	8,056	141,412	5.70%
89	Tamworth	71,310	67,256	869	2,748	437	0	0	4,054	71,310	5.69%
90	Wellingborough	69,992	66,021	0	1,491	2,480	0	0	3,971	69,992	5.67%
91	Liverpool	451,476	426,849	1,108	10,325	10,505	2,689	0	24,627	451,476	5.45%
92	Medway	244,768	231,428	2,652	6,281	3,631	0	776	13,340	244,768	5.45%
93	Spelthorne	88,337	83,526	1,456	1,707	375	0	1,273	4,811	88,337	5.45%
94	Bexley	221,314	209,478	815	3,294	4,177	968	2,582	11,836	221,314	5.35%
95	Dudley	309,216	292,699	2,083	10,610	3,824	0	0	16,517	309,216	5.34%
96	Peterborough	154,829	146,880	2,301	4,693	497	458	0	7,949	154,829	5.13%
97	Southend-on-Sea	175,279	166,406	1,902	2,468	3,568	0	935	8,873	175,279	5.06%
98	Newcastle-under-Lyme	124,414	118,300	1,462	0	0	0	4,652	6,114	124,414	4.91%
99	Stockport	284,566	270,902	2,203	9,757	682	488	534	13,664	284,566	4.80%
100	Kingston upon Hull, City of	240,291	228,761	3,243	2,760	1,088	827	3,612	11,530	240,291	4.80%
101	Gedling	108,916	103,766	0	2,076	2,636	0	438	5,150	108,916	4.73%
102	Redditch	75,591	72,107	0	3,484	0	0	0	3,484	75,591	4.61%
103	Gravesham	90,715	86,555	365	3,795	0	0	0	4,160	90,715	4.59%
104	Tameside	215,243	205,715	3,569	5,437	522	0	0	9,528	215,243	4.43%
105	Stoke-on-Trent	244,811	234,046	3,198	5,909	1,658	0	0	10,765	244,811	4.40%
106	Suffolk Coastal	120,720	115,415	457	0	3,929	919	0	5,305	120,720	4.39%
107	Dartford	82,893	79,254	1,265	458	0	1,916	0	3,639	82,893	4.39%
108	St. Albans	136,887	130,910	866	1,318	1,782	426	1,585	5,977	136,887	4.37%
109	East Hampshire	109,911	105,121	428	0	0	4,362	0	4,790	109,911	4.36%
110	Maldon	60,435	57,808	1,108	380	380	759	0	2,627	60,435	4.35%
111	Broxtowe	108,507	103,832	0	0	2,916	1,759	0	4,675	108,507	4.31%
112	Mid Bedfordshire	127,779	122,315	0	2,851	1,761	426	426	5,464	127,779	4.28%
113	Daventry	70,245	67,259	427	0	0	2,559	0	2,986	70,245	4.25%
114	Epping Forest	119,700	114,637	0	2,088	2,975	0	0	5,063	119,700	4.23%

	District	Total[2]	White	Mixed	Asian or Asian British	Black or Black British	Chinese	Other ethnic group	Total Minority Ethnic inc "Other"[3]	Total of Known Ethnicity[4]	Minority Ethnic %age Known Ethnici
115	Copeland	66,127	63,358	0	2,769	0	0	0	2,769	66,127	4.19%
116	Maidstone	141,069	135,191	1,789	0	744	1,761	1,584	5,878	141,069	4.17%
117	Winchester	109,342	104,809	1,344	3,189	0	0	0	4,533	109,342	4.15%
118	Shepway	103,611	99,353	897	1,684	0	0	1,677	4,258	103,611	4.11%
119	Uttlesford	68,922	66,097	0	2,283	542	0	0	2,825	68,922	4.10%
120	Newcastle upon Tyne	258,941	248,400	1,960	8,018	0	563	0	10,541	258,941	4.07%
121	Middlesbrough	141,933	136,211	0	5,722	0	0	0	5,722	141,933	4.03%
122	Bournemouth	160,859	154,393	1,574	0	963	1,570	2,359	6,466	160,859	4.02%
123	Wyre	106,341	102,075	3,777	0	489	0	0	4,266	106,341	4.01%
124	Hinckley and Bosworth	97,625	93,754	2,251	379	366	875	0	3,871	97,625	3.97%
125	Welwyn Hatfield	95,850	92,056	408	2,160	0	0	1,226	3,794	95,850	3.96%
126	Hart	85,255	81,883	1,212	857	866	437	0	3,372	85,255	3.96%
127	Tonbridge and Malling	108,101	104,011	2,874	0	1,216	0	0	4,090	108,101	3.78%
128	Swindon	179,340	172,556	1,428	4,219	422	395	320	6,784	179,340	3.78%
129	Brighton and Hove	260,086	250,261	1,611	4,815	0	491	2,908	9,825	260,086	3.78%
130	Tunbridge Wells	101,265	97,609	1,161	1,326	1,169	0	0	3,656	101,265	3.61%
131	Rugby	87,718	84,571	0	2,174	973	0	0	3,147	87,718	3.59%
132	South Bucks	63,485	61,280	1,371	421	0	413	0	2,205	63,485	3.47%
133	Adur	58,940	56,920	781	816	0	0	423	2,020	58,940	3.43%
134	Plymouth	252,665	244,015	2,391	1,693	882	425	3,259	8,650	252,665	3.42%
135	East Hertfordshire	126,442	122,131	1,223	1,764	848	476	0	4,311	126,442	3.41%
136	Dacorum	135,281	130,691	683	2,179	1,402	0	326	4,590	135,281	3.39%
137	Runnymede	75,424	72,896	0	567	659	0	1,302	2,528	75,424	3.35%
138	Eastbourne	92,204	89,130	2,230	844	0	0	0	3,074	92,204	3.33%
139	Stockton-on-Tees	188,039	181,896	539	4,819	0	785	0	6,143	188,039	3.27%
140	Portsmouth	182,511	175,513	561	2,017	1,813	1,536	0	5,927	181,440	3.27%
141	South Norfolk	111,862	108,288	2,659	403	0	0	512	3,574	111,862	3.20%
142	Richmondshire	50,527	48,956	1,011	0	0	0	560	1,571	50,527	3.11%
143	Wakefield	319,714	309,836	385	8,610	432	451	0	9,878	319,714	3.09%
144	South Derbyshire	82,310	79,778	796	1,736	0	0	0	2,532	82,310	3.08%
145	West Wiltshire	115,150	111,678	342	0	374	641	2,115	3,472	115,150	3.02%

Appendix C: Ethnic breakdown of the population across unitary and local authority districts

	District	Total[2]	White	Mixed	Asian or Asian British	Black or Black British	Chinese	Other ethnic group	Total Minority Ethnic inc "Other"[3]	Total of Known Ethnicity[4]	Minority Ethnic as %age of Known Ethnicity
146	Exeter	110,825	107,536	1,308	532	0	498	951	3,289	110,825	2.97%
147	Babergh	79,476	77,137	0	488	0	1,851	0	2,339	79,476	2.94%
148	South Cambridgeshire	130,540	126,706	510	592	2,140	0	592	3,834	130,540	2.94%
149	Surrey Heath	84,116	81,754	537	1,825	0	0	0	2,362	84,116	2.81%
150	Broxbourne	86,953	84,517	389	0	1,213	458	376	2,436	86,953	2.80%
151	North Hertfordshire	116,838	113,583	1,132	1,444	679	0	0	3,255	116,838	2.79%
152	Wealden	140,370	136,480	1,496	2,394	0	0	0	3,890	140,370	2.77%
153	South Somerset	155,483	151,300	724	2,159	462	838	0	4,183	155,483	2.69%
154	Bracknell Forest	106,682	103,827	495	1,279	537	0	544	2,855	106,682	2.68%
155	Penwith	62,455	60,787	1,668	0	0	0	0	1,668	62,455	2.67%
156	Mid Sussex	122,254	119,089	0	3,165	0	0	0	3,165	122,254	2.59%
157	Salisbury	112,522	109,618	792	1,675	0	0	437	2,904	112,522	2.58%
158	Vale of White Horse	117,647	114,625	0	2,218	0	0	804	3,022	117,647	2.57%
159	Colchester	161,851	157,737	0	0	1,377	501	2,236	4,114	161,851	2.54%
160	Thurrock	132,630	129,267	3,004	0	359	0	0	3,363	132,630	2.54%
161	Reigate and Banstead	121,607	118,541	1,118	1,160	406	382	0	3,066	121,607	2.52%
162	Dover	109,715	106,957	1,823	0	0	480	455	2,758	109,715	2.51%
163	Doncaster	286,449	279,301	804	3,182	3,162	0	0	7,148	286,449	2.50%
164	East Staffordshire	102,078	99,547	521	2,010	0	0	0	2,531	102,078	2.48%
165	Hartlepool	91,644	89,379	560	0	0	1,705	0	2,265	91,644	2.47%
166	Guildford	129,576	124,653	464	437	533	424	1,285	3,143	127,796	2.46%
167	Woking	94,030	91,745	0	1,546	0	0	739	2,285	94,030	2.43%
168	Great Yarmouth	90,089	87,924	401	1,764	0	0	0	2,165	90,089	2.40%
169	Lichfield	91,258	89,134	1,721	0	403	0	0	2,124	91,258	2.33%
170	East Cambridgeshire	74,078	72,373	804	901	0	0	0	1,705	74,078	2.30%
171	Basildon	168,533	164,681	413	2,089	856	494	0	3,852	168,533	2.29%
172	Crewe and Nantwich	112,604	110,034	0	2,570	0	0	0	2,570	112,604	2.28%
173	Cheltenham	105,036	102,320	0	1,135	0	1,203	0	2,338	104,658	2.23%
174	South Shropshire	41,066	40,170	0	0	0	0	896	896	41,066	2.18%
175	North Lincolnshire	150,568	147,348	0	2,859	0	361	0	3,220	150,568	2.14%
176	Sunderland	284,263	278,218	466	5,265	0	314	0	6,045	284,263	2.13%

Appendix C: Ethnic breakdown of the population across unitary and local authority districts

	District	Total[2]	White	Mixed	Asian or Asian British	Black or Black British	Chinese	Other ethnic group	Total Minority Ethnic inc "Other"[3]	Total of Known Ethnicity[4]	Minority Ethnic %age of Known Ethnicity
177	South Gloucestershire	251,663	246,321	2,800	1,221	819	502	0	5,342	251,663	2.12%
178	Bromsgrove	81,622	79,901	0	1,721	0	0	0	1,721	81,622	2.11%
179	West Oxfordshire	97,869	95,813	448	0	584	0	1,024	2,056	97,869	2.10%
180	Huntingdonshire	157,002	153,718	462	1,977	432	413	0	3,284	157,002	2.09%
181	Rushcliffe	106,879	104,659	401	1,437	382	0	0	2,220	106,879	2.08%
182	Cherwell	140,230	137,440	0	479	1,233	0	1,078	2,790	140,230	1.99%
183	South Tyneside	148,200	145,281	866	1,718	0	0	335	2,919	148,200	1.97%
184	Salford	219,867	215,694	1,748	980	509	484	452	4,173	219,867	1.90%
185	Rotherham	248,151	243,527	1,500	2,372	0	0	752	4,624	248,151	1.86%
186	Wear Valley	59,608	58,507	724	0	0	0	377	1,101	59,608	1.85%
187	Stafford	124,093	121,808	0	1,852	0	433	0	2,285	124,093	1.84%
188	North Cornwall	80,095	78,636	0	1,459	0	0	0	1,459	80,095	1.82%
189	High Peak	90,007	88,378	563	533	0	533	0	1,629	90,007	1.81%
190	West Berkshire	139,984	137,504	1,430	353	0	377	320	2,480	139,984	1.77%
191	Test Valley	110,773	108,823	0	1,596	0	354	0	1,950	110,773	1.76%
192	Solihull	199,450	195,960	0	3,106	384	0	0	3,490	199,450	1.75%
193	Hambleton	85,755	84,276	1,041	0	0	0	438	1,479	85,755	1.72%
194	Amber Valley	121,078	119,072	0	2,006	0	0	0	2,006	121,078	1.66%
195	Eastleigh	120,294	118,322	368	0	1,218	0	386	1,972	120,294	1.64%
196	North Kesteven	95,272	93,744	378	0	0	0	1,150	1,528	95,272	1.60%
197	Ellesmere Port and Neston	76,709	75,482	0	1,227	0	0	0	1,227	76,709	1.60%
198	Norwich	121,726	119,821	999	906	0	0	0	1,905	121,726	1.56%
199	Caradon	80,180	78,953	754	0	473	0	0	1,227	80,180	1.53%
200	Barnsley	223,647	220,325	0	0	2,109	1,213	0	3,322	223,647	1.49%
201	North Dorset	62,968	62,039	428	0	501	0	0	929	62,968	1.48%
202	Nuneaton and Bedworth	117,483	115,782	0	0	1,701	0	0	1,701	117,483	1.45%
203	Harborough	79,017	77,903	533	581	0	0	0	1,114	79,017	1.41%
204	Horsham	123,653	121,259	1,024	349	0	341	0	1,714	122,973	1.39%
205	Harrogate	155,545	153,382	0	0	1,293	435	435	2,163	155,545	1.39%
206	Kerrier	91,730	90,461	1,269	0	0	0	0	1,269	91,730	1.38%

Appendix C: Ethnic breakdown of the population across unitary and local authority districts

	District	Total[2]	White	Mixed	Asian or Asian British	Black or Black British	Chinese	Other ethnic group	Total Minority Ethnic inc "Other"[3]	Total of Known Ethnicity[4]	Minority Ethnic as %age of Known Ethnicity
207	Sedgemoor	104,103	102,665	643	0	795	0	0	1,438	104,103	1.38%
208	Forest Heath	69,993	69,038	0	0	516	0	439	955	69,993	1.36%
209	Halton	118,810	117,189	0	0	1,062	559	0	1,621	118,810	1.36%
210	Erewash	107,304	105,854	724	0	726	0	0	1,450	107,304	1.35%
211	Fenland	81,491	80,394	720	0	377	0	0	1,097	81,491	1.35%
212	North Somerset	193,015	190,488	0	1,238	0	777	512	2,527	193,015	1.31%
213	Lincoln	81,590	80,533	0	1,057	0	0	0	1,057	81,590	1.30%
214	Rutland	37,289	36,815	0	0	0	474	0	474	37,289	1.27%
215	Chelmsford	153,980	152,024	0	0	484	0	1,472	1,956	153,980	1.27%
216	Newark and Sherwood	106,182	104,835	0	1,347	0	0	0	1,347	106,182	1.27%
217	Knowsley	148,762	146,883	1,377	0	0	0	502	1,879	148,762	1.26%
218	Arun	146,592	144,746	0	883	0	963	0	1,846	146,592	1.26%
219	Thanet	127,153	125,552	1,601	0	0	0	0	1,601	127,153	1.26%
220	Rushmoor	82,613	81,586	0	1,027	0	0	0	1,027	82,613	1.24%
221	Worthing	102,836	101,606	390	0	0	428	412	1,230	102,836	1.20%
222	North Wiltshire	123,616	122,167	0	1,449	0	0	0	1,449	123,616	1.17%
223	Canterbury	146,119	144,426	0	0	1,104	0	589	1,693	146,119	1.16%
224	North Devon	88,860	87,870	990	0	0	0	0	990	88,860	1.11%
225	South Staffordshire	100,538	99,444	1,094	0	0	0	0	1,094	100,538	1.09%
226	Blackpool	149,396	147,772	533	0	0	1,091	0	1,624	149,396	1.09%
227	Torbay	128,625	127,227	0	0	0	480	918	1,398	128,625	1.09%
228	Tewkesbury	74,385	73,579	806	0	0	0	0	806	74,385	1.08%
229	Oswestry	34,513	34,147	0	0	366	0	0	366	34,513	1.06%
230	East Riding of Yorkshire	322,342	318,997	852	1,221	832	440	0	3,345	322,342	1.04%
231	Gosport	73,031	72,280	751	0	0	0	0	751	73,031	1.03%
232	Craven	49,605	49,095	0	0	0	0	510	510	49,605	1.03%
233	Hastings	84,383	83,519	864	0	0	0	0	864	84,383	1.02%
234	Forest of Dean	77,481	76,688	340	0	453	0	0	793	77,481	1.02%
235	Tandridge	81,348	80,526	0	411	0	0	411	822	81,348	1.01%
236	Waverley	113,162	111,667	384	0	356	384	0	1,124	112,791	1.00%

	District	Total[2]	White	Mixed	Asian or Asian British	Black or Black British	Chinese	Other ethnic group	Total Minority Ethnic inc "Other"[3]	Total of Known Ethnicity[4]	Minority Ethnic %age of Known Ethnicity
237	Sefton	283,521	280,732	1,235	1,169	0	385	0	2,789	283,521	0.98%
238	Kettering	84,286	83,472	0	814	0	0	0	814	84,286	0.97%
239	North Tyneside	192,454	190,620	396	0	0	1,438	0	1,834	192,454	0.95%
240	South Kesteven	120,154	119,010	331	448	365	0	0	1,144	120,154	0.95%
241	Ashford	106,549	105,538	462	0	549	0	0	1,011	106,549	0.95%
242	Allerdale	91,660	90,796	442	422	0	0	0	864	91,660	0.94%
243	Macclesfield	148,047	146,669	0	0	0	0	1,378	1,378	148,047	0.93%
244	Chester	114,881	113,837	0	526	518	0	0	1,044	114,881	0.91%
245	Mole Valley	79,510	78,389	362	353	0	0	0	715	79,104	0.90%
246	Wirral	327,033	324,131	2,042	422	0	438	0	2,902	327,033	0.89%
247	West Dorset	90,343	89,554	0	405	0	0	384	789	90,343	0.87%
248	Isle of Wight	130,620	128,817	0	0	0	755	363	1,118	129,935	0.86%
249	Melton	48,764	48,347	0	0	0	417	0	417	48,764	0.86%
250	Eden	49,215	48,799	416	0	0	0	0	416	49,215	0.85%
251	Restormel	94,131	93,345	385	0	401	0	0	786	94,131	0.84%
252	Lewes	86,572	85,866	0	0	706	0	0	706	86,572	0.82%
253	St. Edmundsbury	96,412	95,638	387	387	0	0	0	774	96,412	0.80%
254	Bassetlaw	107,351	106,502	0	475	374	0	0	849	107,351	0.79%
255	Corby	49,712	49,333	0	0	379	0	0	379	49,712	0.76%
256	Teignbridge	120,731	119,816	0	413	502	0	0	915	120,731	0.76%
257	Stratford-on-Avon	114,561	113,697	427	0	437	0	0	864	114,561	0.75%
258	Barrow-in-Furness	67,989	67,478	0	0	511	0	0	511	67,989	0.75%
259	Wychavon	114,956	114,118	838	0	0	0	0	838	114,956	0.73%
260	East Northamptonshire	79,038	78,471	0	567	0	0	0	567	79,038	0.72%
261	St. Helens	178,144	176,908	620	616	0	0	0	1,236	178,144	0.69%
262	Weymouth and Portland	60,025	59,612	0	0	0	0	413	413	60,025	0.69%
263	Broadland	121,507	120,693	814	0	0	0	0	814	121,507	0.67%
264	Tendring	137,206	136,302	0	0	416	0	488	904	137,206	0.66%
265	South Northamptonshire	80,287	79,770	0	0	517	0	0	517	80,287	0.64%
266	Redcar and Cleveland	132,812	132,001	0	811	0	0	0	811	132,812	0.61%

Appendix C: Ethnic breakdown of the population across unitary and local authority districts

	District	Total[2]	White	Mixed	Asian or Asian British	Black or Black British	Chinese	Other ethnic group	Total Minority Ethnic inc "Other"[3]	Total of Known Ethnicity[4]	Minority Ethnic as %age of Known Ethnicity
267	East Lindsey	131,749	130,959	392	0	398	0	0	790	131,749	0.60%
268	Congleton	87,475	86,953	0	522	0	0	0	522	87,475	0.60%
269	Castle Point	85,323	84,814	0	0	509	0	0	509	85,323	0.60%
270	Carrick	86,189	85,684	0	505	0	0	0	505	86,189	0.59%
271	Durham	92,448	91,914	0	0	0	534	0	534	92,448	0.58%
272	Scarborough	105,258	104,653	0	0	0	605	0	605	105,258	0.57%
273	York	178,081	177,087	493	0	501	0	0	994	178,081	0.56%
274	Rochford	80,646	80,198	0	0	0	0	448	448	80,646	0.56%
275	Chester-le-Street	56,698	56,384	0	0	0	314	0	314	56,698	0.55%
276	Poole	135,375	134,628	366	0	0	0	381	747	135,375	0.55%
277	South Hams	79,676	79,249	0	427	0	0	0	427	79,676	0.54%
278	Darlington	98,266	97,744	522	0	0	0	0	522	98,266	0.53%
279	Mid Suffolk	85,860	85,404	0	0	0	456	0	456	85,860	0.53%
280	East Dorset	83,749	83,321	0	428	0	0	0	428	83,749	0.51%
281	Staffordshire Moorlands	95,516	95,032	0	0	484	0	0	484	95,516	0.51%
282	North East Lincolnshire	152,231	151,462	0	367	402	0	0	769	152,231	0.51%
283	Gateshead	192,468	191,549	0	507	412	0	0	919	192,468	0.48%
284	Derwentside	84,548	84,160	0	388	0	0	0	388	84,548	0.46%
285	Sevenoaks	111,755	111,264	0	491	0	0	0	491	111,755	0.44%
286	North Norfolk	100,797	100,378	0	0	0	419	0	419	100,797	0.42%
287	Carlisle	98,449	98,064	385	0	0	0	0	385	98,449	0.39%
288	East Devon	128,846	128,377	0	0	0	0	469	469	128,846	0.36%
289	Taunton Deane	100,095	99,735	0	360	0	0	0	360	100,095	0.36%
290	Fareham	105,071	104,697	0	0	374	0	0	374	105,071	0.36%
291	South Bedfordshire	111,325	110,930	0	0	395	0	0	395	111,325	0.35%
292	North East Derbyshire	97,768	97,441	0	327	0	0	0	327	97,768	0.33%
293	King''s Lynn and West Norfolk	134,324	133,889	0	0	0	0	435	435	134,324	0.32%
294	Braintree	139,390	138,993	0	0	0	0	397	397	139,390	0.28%
295	Vale Royal	119,042	118,706	0	336	0	0	0	336	119,042	0.28%
296	Herefordshire, County of	167,964	167,519	0	0	445	0	0	445	167,964	0.26%

Appendix C: Ethnic breakdown of the population across unitary and local authority districts

	District	Total[2]	White	Mixed	Asian or Asian British	Black or Black British	Chinese	Other ethnic group	Total Minority Ethnic inc "Other"[3]	Total of Known Ethnicity[4]	Minority Ethnic %age of Known Ethnicity
297	New Forest	171,523	171,115	408	0	0	0	0	408	171,523	0.24%
298	Alnwick	31,217	31,217	0	0	0	0	0	0	31,217	0.00%
299	Ashfield	107,768	107,768	0	0	0	0	0	0	107,768	0.00%
300	Bath and North East Somerset	171,061	171,061	0	0	0	0	0	0	171,061	0.00%
301	Berwick-upon-Tweed	25,061	25,061	0	0	0	0	0	0	25,061	0.00%
302	Blyth Valley	79,762	79,762	0	0	0	0	0	0	79,762	0.00%
303	Bolsover	71,310	71,310	0	0	0	0	0	0	71,310	0.00%
304	Boston	52,839	52,839	0	0	0	0	0	0	52,839	0.00%
305	Breckland	125,754	125,754	0	0	0	0	0	0	125,754	0.00%
306	Bridgnorth	51,984	51,984	0	0	0	0	0	0	51,984	0.00%
307	Cannock Chase	89,686	89,686	0	0	0	0	0	0	89,686	0.00%
308	Castle Morpeth	50,599	50,599	0	0	0	0	0	0	50,599	0.00%
309	Chesterfield	97,529	97,529	0	0	0	0	0	0	97,529	0.00%
310	Chichester	106,965	106,965	0	0	0	0	0	0	106,965	0.00%
311	Chorley	99,389	99,389	0	0	0	0	0	0	99,389	0.00%
312	Christchurch	42,778	42,778	0	0	0	0	0	0	42,778	0.00%
313	Cotswold	82,515	82,515	0	0	0	0	0	0	82,515	0.00%
314	Derbyshire Dales	71,461	71,461	0	0	0	0	0	0	71,461	0.00%
315	Easington	89,461	89,461	0	0	0	0	0	0	89,461	0.00%
316	Fylde	75,265	75,265	0	0	0	0	0	0	75,265	0.00%
317	Harlow	77,173	77,173	0	0	0	0	0	0	77,173	0.00%
318	Havant	117,826	117,826	0	0	0	0	0	0	117,826	0.00%
319	Kennet	74,365	74,365	0	0	0	0	0	0	74,365	0.00%
320	Lancaster	137,215	137,215	0	0	0	0	0	0	137,215	0.00%
321	Malvern Hills	73,032	73,032	0	0	0	0	0	0	73,032	0.00%
322	Mansfield	98,430	98,430	0	0	0	0	0	0	98,430	0.00%
323	Mendip	101,027	101,027	0	0	0	0	0	0	101,027	0.00%
324	Mid Devon	67,829	67,829	0	0	0	0	0	0	67,829	0.00%
325	North Shropshire	56,528	56,528	0	0	0	0	0	0	56,528	0.00%
326	North Warwickshire	59,460	59,460	0	0	0	0	0	0	59,460	0.00%
327	North West Leicestershire	88,403	88,403	0	0	0	0	0	0	88,403	0.00%

Appendix C: Ethnic breakdown of the population across unitary and local authority districts

	District	Total[2]	White	Mixed	Asian or Asian British	Black or Black British	Chinese	Other ethnic group	Total Minority Ethnic inc "Other"[3]	Total of Known Ethnicity[4]	Minority Ethnic as %age of Known Ethnicity
328	Oadby and Wigston	53,695	53,695	0	0	0	0	0	0	53,695	0.00%
329	Ribble Valley	56,691	56,691	0	0	0	0	0	0	56,691	0.00%
330	Rother	89,882	89,882	0	0	0	0	0	0	89,882	0.00%
331	Ryedale	46,266	46,266	0	0	0	0	0	0	46,266	0.00%
332	Sedgefield	88,425	88,425	0	0	0	0	0	0	88,425	0.00%
333	Selby	71,449	71,449	0	0	0	0	0	0	71,449	0.00%
334	Shrewsbury and Atcham	99,637	99,637	0	0	0	0	0	0	99,637	0.00%
335	South Holland	74,989	74,989	0	0	0	0	0	0	74,989	0.00%
336	South Lakeland	102,621	102,621	0	0	0	0	0	0	102,621	0.00%
337	South Oxfordshire	126,019	126,019	0	0	0	0	0	0	126,019	0.00%
338	South Ribble	105,304	105,304	0	0	0	0	0	0	105,304	0.00%
339	Stroud	108,152	107,782	0	0	0	0	0	0	107,782	0.00%
340	Swale	122,943	122,943	0	0	0	0	0	0	122,943	0.00%
341	Teesdale	25,837	25,837	0	0	0	0	0	0	25,837	0.00%
342	Torridge	55,828	55,828	0	0	0	0	0	0	55,828	0.00%
343	Tynedale	58,229	58,229	0	0	0	0	0	0	58,229	0.00%
344	Wansbeck	59,520	59,520	0	0	0	0	0	0	59,520	0.00%
345	Warrington	187,721	187,721	0	0	0	0	0	0	187,721	0.00%
346	Waveney	111,374	111,374	0	0	0	0	0	0	111,374	0.00%
347	West Devon	47,653	47,653	0	0	0	0	0	0	47,653	0.00%
348	West Lancashire	107,007	107,007	0	0	0	0	0	0	107,007	0.00%
349	West Lindsey	76,255	76,255	0	0	0	0	0	0	76,255	0.00%
350	West Somerset	30,021	30,021	0	0	0	0	0	0	30,021	0.00%
351	Wigan	311,509	311,509	0	0	0	0	0	0	311,509	0.00%
352	Worcester	94,105	94,105	0	0	0	0	0	0	94,105	0.00%
353	Wyre Forest	94,211	94,211	0	0	0	0	0	0	94,211	0.00%
	England	49,588,860	45,234,861	485,443	2,181,313	1,187,002	170,720	313,672	4,338,150	49,573,011	8.75%

1   These data are not directly comparable with Labour Force Survey data quoted in section 6. 'General Population": i) they are from a single quarter (Winter 2000-01), whereas the "General Population" data have been taken from four quarters (Spring 2000 to Winter 2001) and then averaged; and ii) the data sets are based on different ethnic classifications.

2   Includes those who did not state their ethnic origin/question did not apply.

3   "Other ethnic group" is included in the minority ethnic category.

4   "Total of Known Ethnicity" is the sum of the totals for "White", "Mixed", "Asian or Asian British", "Black or Black British", "Chinese" and "Other ethnic group".

(Source: Labour Force Survey 2000-2001)

Appendix D:
Breakdown of student numbers

Student numbers 2000-2001, ethnicity by local LSC						
	LLSC name	White	Minority Ethnic	Total	White %age	Minority Ethnic %age
East of England	LSC Norfolk	36,083	662	36,745	98.2%	1.8%
East of England	LSC Cambridgeshire	40,759	2,966	43,725	93.2%	6.8%
East of England	LSC Suffolk	35,074	1,481	36,555	95.9%	4.1%
East of England	LSC Bedfordshire and Luton	33,482	11,282	44,764	74.8%	25.2%
East of England	LSC Hertfordshire	43,721	6,011	49,732	87.9%	12.1%
East of England	LSC Essex	69,855	4,597	74,452	93.8%	6.2%
East of England		**258,974**	**26,999**	**285,973**	**90.6%**	**9.4%**
East Midlands	LSC Derbyshire	60,169	5,267	65,436	92.0%	8.0%
East Midlands	LSC Nottinghamshire	64,657	10,516	75,173	86.0%	14.0%
East Midlands	LSC Lincolnshire and Rutland	33,325	750	34,075	97.8%	2.2%
East Midlands	LSC Leicestershire	57,827	16,846	74,673	77.4%	22.6%
East Midlands	LSC Northamptonshire	26,903	2,602	29,505	91.2%	8.8%
East Midlands		**242,881**	**35,981**	**278,862**	**87.1%**	**12.9%**
London	LSC London North	33,783	31,988	65,771	51.4%	48.6%
London	LSC London West	31,295	43,267	74,562	42.0%	58.0%
London	LSC London Central	85,422	59,043	144,465	59.1%	40.9%
London	LSC London East	130,207	56,701	186,908	69.7%	30.3%
London	LSC London South	49,595	20,583	70,178	70.7%	29.3%
London		**330,302**	**211,582**	**541,884**	**61.0%**	**39.0%**
North East	LSC Northumberland	14,567	149	14,716	99.0%	1.0%
North East	LSC Tyne and Wear	107,381	6,513	113,894	94.3%	5.7%
North East	LSC County Durham	41,685	702	42,387	98.3%	1.7%
North East	LSC Tees Valley	65,876	2,878	68,754	95.8%	4.2%
North East		**229,509**	**10,242**	**239,751**	**95.7%**	**4.3%**
North West	LSC Cumbria	32,565	491	33,056	98.5%	1.5%
North West	LSC Lancashire	144,725	10,810	155,535	93.0%	7.0%
North West	LSC Greater Merseyside	121,679	5,825	127,504	95.4%	4.6%
North West	LSC Greater Manchester	166,273	28,381	194,654	85.4%	14.6%
North West	LSC Cheshire and Warrington	59,336	1,553	60,889	97.4%	2.6%
North West		**524,578**	**47,060**	**571,638**	**91.8%**	**8.2%**

	LLSC name	White	Minority Ethnic	Total	White %age	Minority Ethnic %age
South East	LSC Milton Keynes, Oxfordshire and Buckinghamshire	52,226	6,313	58,539	89.2%	10.8%
South East	LSC Berkshire	47,407	8,181	55,588	85.3%	14.7%
South East	LSC Hampshire and the Isle of Wight	119,978	5,359	125,337	95.7%	4.3%
South East	LSC Surrey	46,395	4,396	50,791	91.3%	8.7%
South East	LSC Sussex	80,801	5,582	86,383	93.5%	6.5%
South East	LSC Kent and Medway	71,556	5,527	77,083	92.8%	7.2%
South East		**418,363**	**35,358**	**453,721**	**92.2%**	**7.8%**
South West	LSC Devon and Cornwall	121,532	2,483	124,015	98.0%	2.0%
South West	LSC Somerset	44,204	688	44,892	98.5%	1.5%
South West	LSC Bournemouth, Dorset and Poole	37,854	1,584	39,438	96.0%	4.0%
South West	LSC West of England	66,537	6,082	72,619	91.6%	8.4%
South West	LSC Wiltshire and Swindon	41,236	2,303	43,539	94.7%	5.3%
South West	LSC Gloucestershire	43,961	2,470	46,431	94.7%	5.3%
South West		**355,324**	**15,610**	**370,934**	**95.8%**	**4.2%**
West Midlands	LSC Shropshire	39,684	1,458	41,142	96.5%	3.5%
West Midlands	LSC Staffordshire	96,961	3,819	100,780	96.2%	3.8%
West Midlands	LSC The Black Country	49,545	12,752	62,297	79.5%	20.5%
West Midlands	LSC Birmingham and Solihull	84,626	43,714	128,340	65.9%	34.1%
West Midlands	LSC Herefordshire and Worcestershire	53,728	2,101	55,829	96.2%	3.8%
West Midlands	LSC Coventry and Warwickshire	73,856	9,687	83,543	88.4%	11.6%
West Midlands		**398,400**	**73,531**	**471,931**	**84.4%**	**15.6%**
Yorkshire & Humberside	LSC North Yorkshire	43,717	1,002	44,719	97.8%	2.2%
Yorkshire & Humberside	LSC West Yorkshire	117,186	22,828	140,014	83.7%	16.3%
Yorkshire & Humberside	LSC South Yorkshire	87,388	8,618	96,006	91.0%	9.0%
Yorkshire & Humberside	LSC Humberside	71,793	2,375	74,168	96.8%	3.2%
Yorkshire & Humberside		**320,084**	**34,823**	**354,907**	**90.2%**	**9.8%**
		3,078,415	491,186	3,569,601	86.2%	13.8%

Source ISR20fe.   Coverage of Institutes = 92%

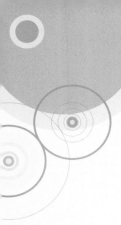

Appendix E:
Recruitment and selection of Black staff

Outlined below are findings from the Learning and Skills Development Agency and the Commission for Black Staff in Further Education research, *Black issues in recruitment procedures and processes in the Further Education sector,* (London, April 2002).

Positive indicators

- A high proportion of colleges had recruitment and selection procedures that reflected acknowledged good practice.

- Some involvement of Black and minority ethnic staff on recruitment panels was taking place – there were also examples of colleges bringing in external expertise to ensure racial equality in the recruitment process.

- Some colleges targeted under-represented talent through links with external sources.

- More job opportunities were being advertised through a variety of media, including the minority ethnic press.

- Some Black senior managers acted as mentors and role models to support the personal development of other staff.

- Most colleges had staff induction programmes and appraisal systems.

Emerging concerns

- Minority ethnic staff were under-represented at all levels.

- There was a lack of knowledge and awareness about diversity issues.

- There was a lack of effective staff development in interviewing skills and processes.

- There was a lack of guidance on how to remove barriers to equity in recruitment, selection and induction, for example, in the compilation of job and person specifications or the use of recruitment agencies.

- There were examples of staff involvement on recruitment and selection panels when they had not been part of the initial shortlisting process.

- There was a lack of formal written guidelines for complaints and appeals procedures in the selection process.

- The effectiveness of mentorship, work-shadowing and other support and development interventions was questioned and needed further exploration.

- There was a lack of local benchmarking and comparative data to enable colleges to set targets and monitor staff profiles.

Appendix F:
Ethnicity and employment
in higher education

Below is a summary of findings from research into ethnicity and employment in higher education (Carter J, Fenton, S and Modood, T (1999) *Ethnicity and Employment in Higher Education*, London: Policy Studies Institute.)

- Approximately 6.5% of academic staff in UK higher education institutions were not White; just over half of these were non-British nationals.

- Bangladeshi, Pakistani, Black Caribbean and 'Black Other' were significantly under-represented in academic posts; Chinese, 'Asian Other' and Indian ethnic groups accounted for approximately three quarters of all who were not White.

- Minorities were on average younger and had shorter lengths of service and they were less likely to be professors.

- Non-British nationality staff (White and minority ethnic) were highly concentrated in research posts. Minority ethnic staff were more likely to be in research-only posts than majority ethnic staff.

- Women in all groups were under-represented in academic posts and were more likely to be on fixed-term contract, part-time less senior posts. Minority ethnic women, especially non-British were the most disadvantaged.

The survey found that:

- A third of institutions did not have a racial equality policy.

- Three quarters of all institutions said they monitored job applications by ethnicity, but only 30% stated that any policy decisions had been made on the basis of these statistics.

- Only 26% of institutions monitored internal promotions.

- Only 5% of the sample said they had a positive action plan for minority ethnic groups.

- About one in five minority ethnic respondents said they had personally experienced discrimination in job applications or in promotion and had experienced racial harassment from staff or students.

- Thirty per cent of minority ethnic respondents said they felt they had been discriminated against in job applications.

- A large proportion of respondents, including White staff, said they were unsure about their institution's commitment to equal opportunities.

- Fifty-five per cent of British minorities and 49% of non-British minorities believed 'greatly' or 'partly' that discrimination in employment in higher education existed. Although 19% of White staff did not express this view, 41% were 'not sure'.

- Minority staff and research students said they resented being typecast by their ethnicity, nationality or gender.

Appendix G:
Expert witnesses

Name and title of person invited	Organisation
Nick Montague Head of Regulatory Reform Action Team, Regulatory Impact Unit	Cabinet Office
Joe Charlesworth Policy Officer: Local Government – Further & Higher Education, Learning & Skills Councils	Commission for Racial Equality (CRE)
Bob Purkiss Commissioner	Commission for Racial Equality (CRE)
Peter Mucklow Divisional Manager for FE Partnerships Division	Department for Education and Employment (now DfES)
Chris Hughes Chief Executive	Further Education Development Agency (now LSDA)
Liz Walker Development Advisor	Further Education Development Agency (now LSDA)
Adjei Burwuah Development Adviser	Further Education Development Agency (now LSDA)
Trevor Hall Team Leader in Qualifications for Work Division	Home Office
Stella Dadzie F.E. Consultant	Front Line Training
Jim Thakoordin F.E. Consultant	F.E. Consultant
William Gulam H.E. Consultant	F.E. Consultant
Trevor Gordon Head of Equal Opportunity Services	Lambeth College
Harbhajan Singh Brar Human Resources Director	Lewisham College
John Harwood Chief Executive	Learning & Skills Council (LSC)
Emer Clarke Assistant Director of Quality Improvement	Learning & Skills Council (LSC)
Jim Donaldson Chief Inspector	Further Education Funding Council (FEFC)
Steven Grix Head of Post 16 Division	Office for Standards in Education (OFSTED)
Dr John Carter Research Lectureship	Oxford Brooks University
Sandy Wilson Professional Officer, Teacher Supply & Recruitment	Teacher Training Agency
David Sherlock Chief Executive	Training Standards Council
Roger MacKenzie Policy Officer for Equal Rights Department	Trades Union Congress (TUC)
Paul Mackney General Secretary	National Association of Teachers in Further & Higher Education (NATFHE)
Midge Purcell PR Official/Co-Editor	National Association of Teachers in Further & Higher Education (NATFHE)
Wilf Sullivan Black Members Officer	UNISON

Glossary of key terms

Black

Black is commonly used to describe people who because of their 'race', colour or ethnic origin are identifiably different. Originally used to refer exclusively to people of African descent, it now also serves as an umbrella term and may include people from a much wider range of geographic, cultural and linguistic backgrounds. When used in this generic way, 'Black' refers to people with a common yet diverse experience of racism rather than a particular skin tone. The Commission has used the generic term 'Black' to refer to members of African, African Caribbean, Asian and other visible minority ethnic communities who may face racism. However, the Commission is conscious that the debate on terminology is constantly developing.

Culture

Culture refers to the shared rituals, symbols and practices that give a group its sense of identity. Expressed through music, language, food, dress, art etc, culture is a dynamic concept that may include, but is not necessarily the same as, someone's personal beliefs or their religious or moral values.

Direct discrimination

Direct race discrimination occurs when a person is treated less favourably than others on grounds of their race. The Race Relations Act defines 'racial grounds' as race, colour or nationality (including citizenship), and ethnic or national origins (RRA 1(1)(a)). People from all racial groups, including White people, are protected by this law.

Ethnic minority/minority ethnic

Ethnic minority refers to people who belong to minority groups with a distinct cultural and historical identity. The term is used loosely to encompass:

- people who were born overseas but have settled in Britain
- people who are British born whose parents or grandparents were born overseas
- religious and linguistic minorities
- national minorities like the Welsh, Irish or Scottish.

The term 'minority ethnic' reverses the emphasis in order to stress that all people belong to ethnic groups. Thus people are described as belong to majority or minority ethnic groups. These terms may need to be reviewed as in

some inner-city areas 'minority' ethnic groups are increasingly likely to be in the numerical majority.

Ghettoisation

The term 'ghettoisation' refers to the clustering of Black staff or students in certain geographic or vocational areas of the college – for example, ESOL or Community Outreach – in a way that confirms stereotypical assumptions about what Black staff or students do best.

Harassment

Harassment on grounds of race involves threatening, intrusive or undermining behaviour towards a person of a particular racial or ethnic group. It is usually, though not always, intentional and on-going. It includes persistent name-calling, bullying or ridicule, and acts of psychological, verbal or physical abuse.

Indirect discrimination

Indirect discrimination on grounds of race occurs when a criterion or apparently neutral practice which applies equally to everyone has a disproportionately adverse effect on people from a particular racial group, and there is no objective justification for the rule (RRA 1(1)(b), 28). The definition changed in line with the EC Burden of Proof Directive that came into force in July 2000.

Institutional racism

Institutional racism, as defined by Macpherson, refers to 'the collective failure of an organisation to provide an appropriate and professional service to people because of their colour, culture or ethnic origin … seen or detected in processes, attitudes and behaviour which amount to discrimination through unwitting prejudice, ignorance, thoughtlessness and racist stereotyping which disadvantage minority ethnic people'. While this kind of racism may be unconscious or unwitting, as Macpherson suggests, there is evidence that it can also be calculated and deliberate.

Marginalisation

Marginalisation occurs when a person or group is excluded from decision-making or mainstream activities.

Positive action

It is lawful under both the Race Relations and the Sex Discrimination Acts to provide training and special encouragement for people of a particular racial group, or either sex, who have been under-represented in certain occupations or grades during the previous 12 months (RRA 37, 38; SDA 47). It is also lawful to address any special educational, training or welfare needs identified for a specific racial group (RRA 35). Positive action encompasses a range of measures to encourage people to take full and equal advantage of opportunities in jobs, education and training. It is not to be confused with positive or 'reverse' discrimination, which involves giving preferential treatment to a particular group and which remains illegal in the UK.

Prejudice

Prejudice occurs when someone pre-judges an individual or group of people from a particular racial group because of ignorance or a belief in certain stereotypes or assumptions.

'Race'

The idea that people belong to different races was developed in the 18th and 19th centuries in an attempt to explain perceived differences between people. However, genetic research has shown that a person's skin colour is of little more relevance than the colour of their eyes or hair. The notion of 'race' is used less often these days as genetic research has shown that biologically, human beings are essentially the same. Recent studies also suggest that prior miscegenation (the mixing of people from different racial groups) is common within three or four generations, even in individuals who, from their appearance, are identified as White, Black or Asian.

Racism

Racism describes a complex set of attitudes and behaviour towards people from another racial or minority ethnic group resulting from long-standing historical relationships. It is most commonly based on:

- the belief that physical or cultural differences correspond directly with differences in personality, intelligence or ability, leading to assumptions about racial superiority or inferiority

- the social and economic power of members of one racial or ethnic group to promote or enforce such attitudes

- racism is described in the Macpherson report as both overt and subtle '… conduct … words or practices which advantage or disadvantage people because of their colour, culture or ethnic origin.'

Stereotyping

Stereotyping is the act of labelling or categorising particular groups, usually in a negative way, because of pre-conceived ideas. It relies on broad generalisations, often popularly held, that all members of a particular racial or ethnic group will think and behave identically.

Structural racism

Structural racism describes discrimination that is endemic within wider society – for example, in education, employment, housing and the criminal justice system. It goes beyond individual organisations, referring to the way racism has come to pervade the culture and institutions of British society as a whole.

Tokenism

Tokenism refers to the appointment or use of individuals in positions that carry little or no influence, conveying the false impression that they have power or status within the organisation.

Victimisation

Victimisation on grounds of race occurs when a person is discriminated against for taking action under the Race Relations Act or for supporting such action by another (RRA2). A recent ruling by the House of Lords makes it clear that an employer can be found liable regardless of whether they are consciously or subconsciously motivated.

Visible minority

Visible minority is an alternative term for 'ethnic minority'. Some see it as a less ambiguous way of identifying non-White groups.

Bibliography

Association of Colleges (2002) *FE Now*, The Independent.

Carter J, Fenton, S and Modood, T (1999) *Ethnicity and Employment in Higher Education*, London: Policy Studies Institute.

Commission for Black Staff in Further Education (2002) *Summary report: an agenda for action,* London.

Commission for Racial Equality (2001) *Ethnic monitoring: A guide for public authorities*, London.

Commission for Racial Equality (2002) *Framework for a race equality for further education colleges*, London.

Department for Education and Employment press notice (4 April 2001/0193).

Dickens, R, Gregg, P and Wadsworth J (2001) *The State of Working Britain, York*: York Publishing.

Dominelli (second ed. 1998:7) *Anti-racist social work*, London: MacMillan.

Equal Opportunity Commission, *Equality in the 21st century, Annual Report 1999/2000*.

Farish, M, McPake, J, Powney, J and Weiner, G (1995) *Equal Opportunties in Colleges and Universities: Towards Better Practices*, Buckingham: SRHE and the Open University Press.

Further Education Funding Council, *National Report from the Inspectorate 1999 – 2000: Supporting Part-Time Teachers in Further Education*.

The Guardian (1995) 20 June.

Harvard Business Review (April 2001).

HM Treasury (2002) *Developing workforce skills: piloting a new approach* London.

Labour Research Department (2002) *Labour Research, April*.

Learning and Skills Council, *Individualised Student Record 20, 2000-2001*.

Learning and Skills Council (2002) *National Equality and Diversity Strategy*.

Learning and Skills Council, *Staff Individualised Record 9, 2000-01*.

Learning and Skills Council, *Widening participation in further education – statistical evidence, 1999-2000*.

Learning and Skills Development Agency and the Commission for Black Staff in Further Education (April 2002) *Black issues in recruitment procedures and processes in the Further Education sector*, London.

Macpherson, W (1999) *The Stephen Lawrence Inquiry: Report of an Inquiry by Sir William Macpherson*, London: Stationery Office.

NATFHE (2002) *Overworked and undervalued*, London.

The Observer (2002) 28 April.

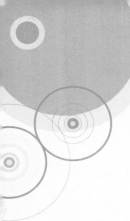

Office for National Statistics, *Labour Force Survey 2000-2001.*

Office for National Statistics, *Regional trends 36 – 2001 Edition.*

ORC International (2001) *Association of Colleges and joint unions national review of staffing and pay in further education*, London.

Owen, D et al (2000) *Minority Ethnic Participation and Achievements in Education, Training and the Labour Market* Research Brief, DfEE.

Rampton, A (1981) *West Indian Children in our Schools: Interim Report of the Committee of Inquiry into the Education of Children from Ethnic Minority Groups,* Series: Cmnd., 8273, London: HMSO.

Rushanara and O' Cinneide (2002) *Our House? Race and representation in British Politics*, London: Institute for Public Policy Research.

Swann, M, B (1985) *Education for All: The Report of the Committee of Enquiry into the Education of Children from Ethnic Minority Groups*, presented to Parliament by the Secretary for Education and Science Series: Cmnd. 9453, London: HMSO.

The Times (2002) 26 April.

Times Educational Supplement (2001) 16 November.

Times Educational Supplement (2002) 4 January.

V E.L. LEARNING RESOURCES